16.90

DAILY LIFE

A SOURCEBOOK ON COLONIAL AMERICA

DAILY LIFE

A SOURCEBOOK ON COLONIAL AMERICA

Edited by Carter Smith

AMERICAN ALBUMS FROM THE COLLECTIONS OF
THE LIBRARY OF CONGRESS

THE MILLBROOK PRESS, *Brookfield, Connecticut*

Cover: Second Street, north from Market Street, with Christ Church, Philadelphia (detail), etching and engraving by William and Thomas Birch, 1798-1800.

Title Page: Farmyard scene, engraving from Massachusetts Magazine, *1796.*

Contents Page: "A Bird in the Hand is worth Two in the Bush," woodcut from Benjamin Franklin's Poor Richard's Almanack, *eighteenth century.*

Back Cover: "Preparation for War to Defend Commerce," etching and engraving by William and Thomas Birch, 1798-1800.

Library of Congress Cataloging-in-Publication Data

Daily life : a sourcebook on colonial America / edited by Carter Smith.
p. cm. -- (American albums from the collections of the Library of Congress)
Includes bibliographical references and index.
Summary: Describes and illustrates daily life in colonial America through a variety of images produced at the time.
ISBN 1-56294-038-4
1. United States--Social life and customs--Colonial period, ca. 1600-1775--Juvenile literature. 2. United States--Social life and customs--Colonial period, ca. 1600-1775--Sources--Juvenile literature. 3. United States--Social life and customs--Colonial period, ca. 1600-1775--Pictorial works--Juvenile literature. [1. United States--Social life and customs--Colonial period, ca. 1600-1775--Sources.] I. Smith, C. Carter. II. Series.
E162.D15 1991
973.2--dc20 91-13941
CIP
AC

Created in association with Media Projects Incorporated

C. Carter Smith, *Executive Editor*
Lelia Wardwell, *Managing Editor*
Charles A. Wills, *Consulting Editor*
Kimberly Horstman, *Researcher*
Lydia Link, *Designer*
Athena Angelos, *Photo Researcher*

The consultation of Bernard F. Reilly, Jr., Head Curator of the Prints and Photographs Division of the Library of Congress, is gratefully acknowledged.

Manufactured in the United States of America.

10 9 8 7 6 5 4 3 2 1

Contents

A Bird in the Hand is worth two in the Bufh.

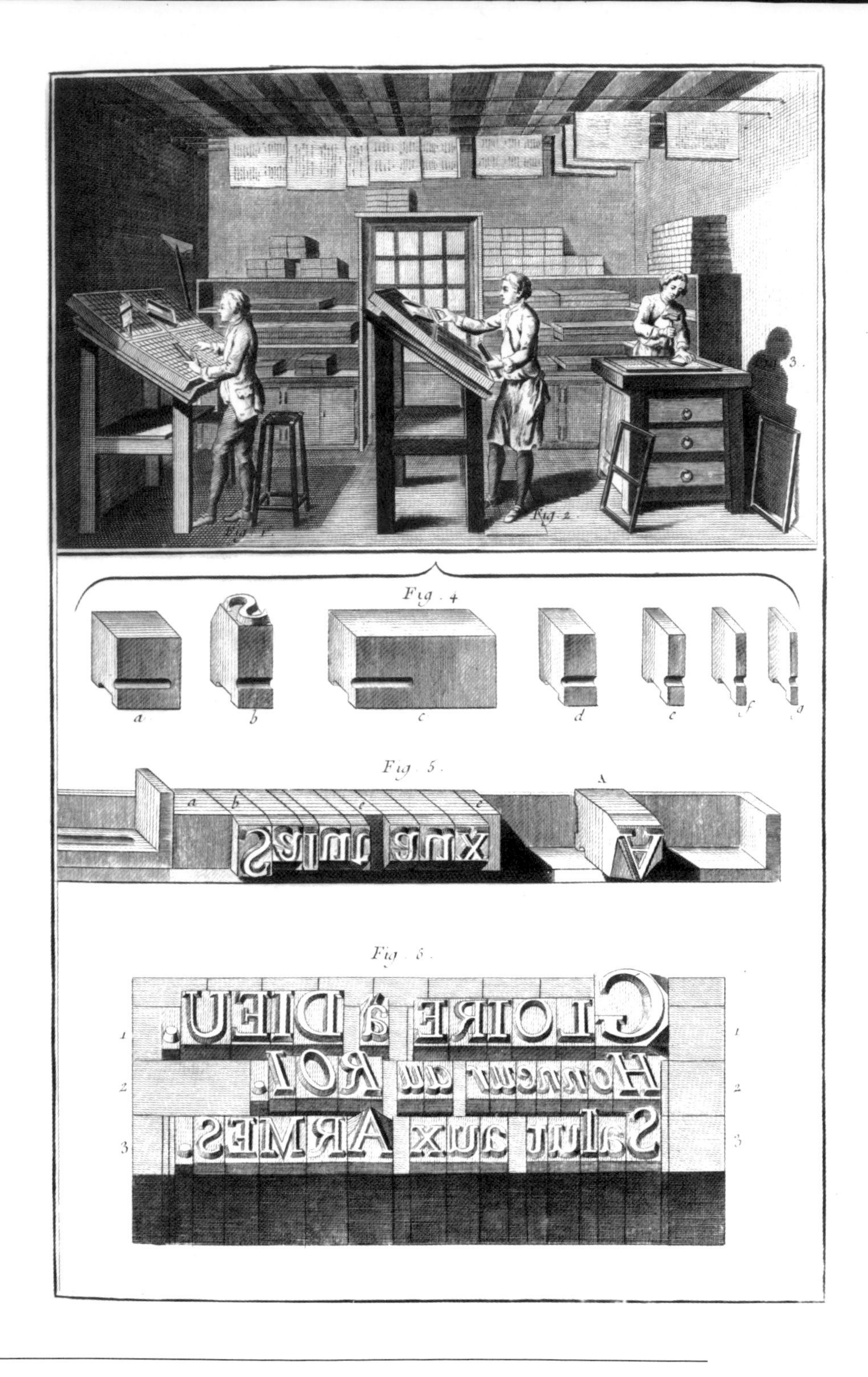

Printing was an important business in colonial cities and towns, where reading and writing were especially valued. This copperplate engraving from Denis Diderot's Encyclopédie des Arts et des Métiers (Encyclopedia of Trades and Industry) *shows the composing room of a print shop. The typesetter (farthest left) is arranging the letters in a typecase while another worker (figure 2) is forming the text into pages.*

Introduction

DAILY LIFE is one of the initial volumes in a series published by the Millbrook Press titled AMERICAN ALBUMS FROM THE COLLECTIONS OF THE LIBRARY OF CONGRESS, and one of six books in the series subtitled SOURCEBOOKS ON COLONIAL AMERICA. They treat the early history of our homeland from its discovery and early settlement through the colonial and Revolutionary wars.

The editors' basic goal for the series is to make available to the student many of the original visual documents preserved in the Library of Congress as records of the American past. DAILY LIFE reproduces many of the prints, broadsides, maps, and other original works preserved in the Library's special collections divisions, and a few from its general book collections.

Given particular prominence in this volume are the rich holdings of eighteenth century illustrated magazines, almanacs, scientific books, and technical manuals preserved in the Library's Rare Book and Special Collections Division. In the predominantly agricultural society of colonial America, journals like the *Columbian* and *Massachusetts* magazines were invaluable sources for new farming, husbandry, and manufacturing methods. Such journals were eagerly read by the farmers and gentlemen planters of the colonies. They provided the outlines of manufacturing processes, such as that in the *Massachusetts Magazine* of the various stages of wool production, which were particularly useful to the sheep and livestock producers which served these industries. Engravings of designs for such practical structures as the more efficient grain elevator portrayed in the *Columbian Magazine* kept colonists current with innovations from their neighbors and from the Old World. Likewise the almanac literature served the smaller, subsistence farmer, and provided him with a wealth of practical information and inspiration as well.

In a similar way, the encyclopedias and pattern books of the eighteenth century (most of which were produced in Britain and France) served as guides to colonial craftsmen. Diderot's monumental illustrated *Encyclopédie* was a boon to the industries and trades of Enlightenment Europe and America, providing an unprecedented sharing of technology, previously disseminated much more slowly and guardedly through the guild system.

Today the woodcuts and engravings which appeared in these publications give us a good sense of the ways in which the American colonial farmers and craftsmen went about their work, and of the means by which the trades and crafts of the eighteenth century evolved toward the roaring industry of the nineteenth. The works reproduced here represent a small but telling portion of the rich record of daily life and work in the colonial period, preserved by the Library of Congress in its role as the nation's library.

BERNARD F. REILLY, JR.

A TIMELINE OF MAJOR EVENTS

1490-1599

WORLD HISTORY

Columbus sets out for America

1492 Spain is finally united under Ferdinand and Isabella; the nation is now able to devote attention to exploration. Christopher Columbus claims North America for Spain.

1517 German monk Martin Luther protests abuses in the Roman Catholic Church, beginning the Protestant Reformation.

1520 Ferdinand Magellan, a Portuguese explorer and navigator sailing for Spain, reaches the Pacific Ocean by sailing through the straits named after him at the foot of the South American continent. He is killed in the Philippine Islands the next year.

1534 The English Parliament passes the Act of Supremacy acknowledging Henry VIII as head of the Church of England, beginning the English Reformation.

1559 Elizabeth I becomes Queen of England.

1569 Gerardus Mercator publishes the first cylindrical world map showing longitude, latitude, and the equator.

1588 The Spanish Armada sails from Spain hoping to invade and conquer England; the fleet is destroyed by a combination of English warships and storms.

AMERICAN HISTORY GOVERNMENT

1494 Pope Alexander VI issues the Treaty of Tordesillas, dividing the New World between Spain and Portugal.

Pope Alexander VI

1512 Spain issues the Laws of Burgos, which are designed to protect Indians from cruel treatment in Spain's colonies.

1518 Charles V, King of Spain and the Holy Roman Emperor, allows African slaves to be sent to the New World.

1532 To strengthen its colonies, the Spanish government requires ships sailing to the New World to carry livestock and seeds for crops.

1542 The Spanish government ends the practice of *encomienda*, a system that allowed colonists to tax New World Indians or force them to work.

1570 Five Indian tribes in northeastern North America join together to form the Iroquois Confederacy.

Totem of the Five Nations of the Iroquois Confederacy

1583 Sir Humphrey Gilbert is granted a patent to colonize North America by Queen Elizabeth of England.

AMERICAN HISTORY SOCIETY AND INDUSTRY

1514 Spain institutes the *Requerimiento*, a law requiring all Indians in Spain's New World possessions to convert to Christianity or face slavery or death.

1517 Bartolomé de Las Casas, a Spanish priest, urges better treatment of the native population in Spain's New World; he becomes the first Catholic priest ordained in the New World.

Bartolomé de Las Casas

1540 Four Francisan friars accompany Coronado's expedition through southwestern North America.

1544 Spanish friar Juan de Padilla is killed by Indians in what is now New Mexico, becoming the first missionary to die in what will later be known as the United States.

1499-1599 Relations between Native Americans and Spanish, French, and English explorers and settlers vary from region to region. While Native Americans and colonists sometimes try to cooperate, the increasing numbers of European settlers lead to widespread suffering, death, and enslavement for much of the New World's Native American population.

John Smith clashing with the Indians

1600-1649

1603 Queen Elizabeth I of England dies. She is succeeded by James VI, who unites the thrones of England and Scotland and rules as James I.

1605 Spanish author Miguel de Cervantes publishes Part I of his novel, *Don Quixote de la Mancha*.

1611 A new English translation of the Bible, authorized by King James, is published.

William Shakespeare

1616 Poet and playwright William Shakespeare, greatest writer of the Elizabethan era and probably in all English literature, dies at his home in Stratford-upon-Avon.

1618 The Thirty Years War begins, originally between Protestants and Catholics in central Europe.

1630-42 Some 16,000 colonists from England emigrate to Massachusetts.

1637 Russian explorers reach the Pacific Ocean, having crossed Siberia.

1642 The English Civil War begins; it is a conflict between supporters of Charles I and the Church of England and the largely Puritan supporters of Parliamentary government led by Oliver Cromwell. Many supporters of the king emigrate to America. •Montreal is founded by the French.

1643 Louis XIV, the "Sun King," begins a seventy-two-year reign as king of France.

1606 James I of England charters two companies, the Plymouth Company and the Virginia Company, to establish colonies in North America.

1607 The Jamestown Colony is founded; the settlement is governed by a council under the supervision of the Virginia Company in England.

1619 The first elected assembly in English North America—the Virginia House of Burgesses—holds its first session at Jamestown.

Seal of the Virginia Company

1620 The Pilgrims sign the Mayflower Compact while still aboard the *Mayflower*, binding the signers to obey "just and equal laws."

1623 "According to the commendable custom of England," the Pilgrims establish trial by twelve-man jury at Plymouth.

1635 A Maryland Indian leader protests the colony's insistence the Indians obey English law; instead, he suggests the Colonists "conform to the customs of our country."

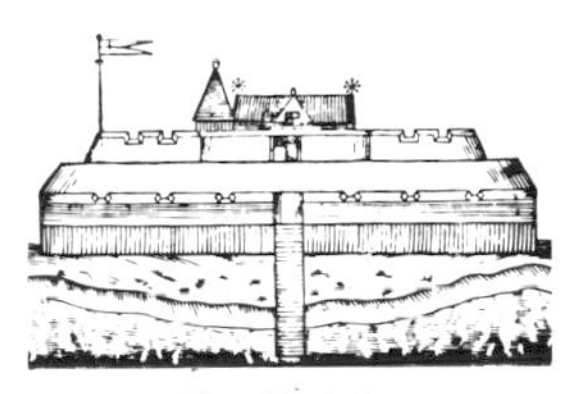

Fort Christina

1638 Swedish colonists found Fort Christina near what is now Wilmington, Delaware.

1606 Bishop Juan de la Cabezade de Altimirano visits St. Augustine, Florida. He is the first bishop to set foot in North America.

1608 John Smith's account of life in Virginia is the first book from the colonies to be published in London.

1610 A new law compels the Jamestown settlers to attend church.

1612 John Rolfe establishes what will become the most important cash crop of the southern English colonies by cultivating new varieties of tobacco.

1614 Pocahontas, the

Pocahontas

seventeen-year-old daughter of Indian leader Powhatan, is baptized as a Christian (with the name Rebecca), and marries John Rolfe at the Jamestown settlement in Virginia.

1615 Franciscan missionaries arrive in Quebec.

1620 Seeking religious freedom, the Pilgrims sail from England for Virginia. They make landfall at Cape Cod and later found a colony at Plymouth, Massachusetts.

1621 In November, the Plymouth settlers celebrate their first anniversary in the colony with a feast of Thanksgiving.

1622 One-fourth of the Jamestown colonists, 357 people, die in an attack by the Powhatan Indians, which begins two years of war.

A TIMELINE OF MAJOR EVENTS

1650-1674

WORLD HISTORY

1651 Charles II, son of Charles I, is crowned king of Scotland; after unsuccessfully invading England, he flees to France.

1652 England declares war on Holland.

1654 The Treaty of Westminster ends the first Anglo-Dutch War.

1658 French and English forces defeat the Spanish at the Battle of the Dunes near Dunkirk. The Peace of the Pyrenees, signed the next year, sets the Spanish border at the Pyrenees Mountains.

1660 The monarchy is restored in England, with Charles II as king.

1666 London is almost destroyed by the "Great Fire," which starts in a bakery.

The Great Fire of London

1667 France invades the Spanish Netherlands.

1672 William of Orange (later William III of England) is made Captain-General of the United Provinces (the Netherlands).

•England's Royal African Company wins exclusive right to capture African slaves for sale in the New World. The monopoly covers the African coast from Morocco to the Cape of Good Hope.

AMERICAN HISTORY

GOVERNMENT

1650 England's first Navigation Act gives the nation's merchants a monopoly on trade with its colonies; the law also requires colonists to sell their products only to England and to ship them aboard English vessels.

1651 The colonies are caught up in the English Civil War. In Virginia, Governor William Berkeley is forced to surrender to a Parliamentary fleet.

1652 Massachusetts declares itself a self-governing commonwealth; New England, being mostly Puritan, supports the Parliamentary cause in England.

1653 Peter Stuyvesant allows some local government in New Amsterdam, but says his power to rule "comes from God and the company, not a few ignorant citizens."

1658 The first colonial police force is organized in New Amsterdam.

1660 Virginia passes the first of many laws defining the status of slavery and depriving slaves of legal rights; most other colonies adopt similar "slave codes." Dutch traders had brought the first slaves to Virginia in 1619.

1670 The great political philosopher John Locke writes the Fundamental Constitutions, setting up the legal framework for English settlements in the Carolinas.

John Locke

AMERICAN HISTORY

SOCIETY AND INDUSTRY

1652 Rhode Island bans slavery, but the law is not enforced.

•Although Britain forbids the colonies from producing their own money, Massachusetts mints the first colonial coin, the Pine Tree shilling.

1653 New Amsterdam (later New York City) incorporates as a city with over 800 residents.

A Pine Tree shilling

1656 Mohawk Indians ask the Dutch to outlaw the sale of rum to Indians.

1665 There are now some 75,000 English colonists in the New World. French settlers number about 3,500.

•In Accomack, Virginia, two actors are charged with "excessive frivolity" for their roles in the first play ever staged in the colonies, *Ye Bare and Ye Cubb*. The charges are dismissed, and the plaintiff is ordered to pay court costs.

1670 A Boston tavern offers a new drink: chocolate, a beverage of Mexican Indian origin. It came to the colonies from the West Indies.

1673 England appoints customs officers and authorizes its navy to enforce new laws imposing duty on goods shipped between the colonies.

• Mail can now be delivered between Boston and New York by relays of riders stationed along the so-called "Post Road."

1675-1699

1678 Rumors of a "Popish Plot" to restore Catholicism in England lead to anti-Catholic persecutions and laws.

1685 Louis XIV of France revokes the Edict of Nantes, renewing conflict between French Catholics and Protestants.

1686 Catholic European nations join together as the League of Augsburg to oppose France's plans for expansion.

King Louis XIV

1688 In the bloodless "Glorious Revolution," England's Catholic King James II is overthrown; he is replaced by his Protestant Dutch son-in-law William III, who rules jointly with Queen Mary.

1689 The English Parliament passes a Declaration of Rights, limiting royal power and prohibiting Catholics from ruling.
•Peter the Great becomes czar of Russia and brings European ideas and technology to that nation.
•The War of the Grand Alliance breaks out, pitting France against the coalition of states (including England and Spain) that make up the League of Augsburg.

1697 The Treaty of Ryswick ends the War of the Grand Alliance; there is no clear winner, but France gives up some territory.

King Philip

1675 King Philip's War, between English colonists and Native American tribes in Massachusetts, Rhode Island, and Connecticut, causes damage or destruction in sixty-four colonial towns and destroys many Indian villages.

1682 After almost two years of traveling the Mississippi River, René Robert Cavelier, sieur de La Salle, reaches the river's mouth and claims all the land along its banks—a territory he names Louisiana.

•William Penn founds Philadelphia and the Pennsylvania colony as a refuge for Quakers and other persecuted religious minorities.

1687 To assert the Crown's authority, Royal Governor Sir Edmund Andros demands Connecticut's original charter. According to some accounts, colonists hide the charter in a hollow oak tree in Hartford to frustrate Andros.

1696 Parliament passes another Navigation Act, setting up a board of trade to oversee commerce with the colonies.

1697 William Penn proposes a congress with representatives from all the colonies.

1699 Virginia's capital is moved from Jamestown to Williamsburg.

1675 The Massachusetts General Court says that recent Indian attacks are due to the sinfulness of some colonists, including men who wear their hair as long as a woman's.

1679 French explorer René Robert Cavelier, sieur de La Salle, discovering the commercial possibilities of the frontier, sends a ship loaded with furs from Green Bay (Wisconsin) to Fort Niagara in New York.

1680 In Virginia, John Banister writes the first study of North American plants.

1682 William Penn plans Philadelphia on the "gridiron" pattern later adopted by many American cities. The lots he offers are big enough for a garden and an orchard.

1690 The first paper mill in the colonies is established in Pennsylvania.

1692 Twenty men and women are executed for witchcraft in Salem, Massachusetts.

1693 A new postal service links Portsmouth, New Hampshire, with Boston.

Boston post-boy

1697 New York becomes the first city in the colonies to employ paid firefighters.

1699 A yellow fever epidemic kills one-sixth of Philadelphia's population.
•Brothers Pierre and Jacques Le Moyne establish Old Biloxi, now known as Ocean Springs, Mississippi, the first of several French settlements along the Gulf of Mexico.

A TIMELINE OF MAJOR EVENTS

1700-1724

WORLD HISTORY

1701 The question of who will rule Spain and its empire leads to the War of the Spanish Succession; eventually, Spain and France are opposed by England, Holland, and several other states.
•Frederick, ruler of Brandenburg, becomes the first king of Prussia.

The Duke of Marlborough

1704 Forces led by England's Duke of Marlborough win a major victory over France and Spain in the Battle of Blenheim.

1713 The Treaty of Utrecht ends the War of the Spanish Succession.

1714 Queen Anne of England dies and is succeeded by the German George I, elector of Hanover and a great-grandson of James I.

1718 England declares war on Spain; France follows a year later.

1720 France's treasury is bankrupted after the Mississippi Company is revealed to be a sham.

Seal of the Mississippi Company

1722 Dutch explorer Jacob Roggeveen discovers a remote island in the Pacific Ocean, on Easter Sunday, and names it Easter Island.

AMERICAN HISTORY GOVERNMENT

1702 Delaware sets up a government separate from Pennsylvania.
•Queen Anne's War (in Europe called the War of the Spanish Succession) brings fighting in Canada between French and English colonists.

1704 The New York Assembly seizes power from the royal governor.

1712 North Carolina separates from South Carolina and gets its own governor.

1716 Virginia governor Alexander Spotswood leads an expedition into the westernmost Virginia territory, crossing the Blue Ridge Mountains into the Shenandoah River valley.

1718 The French under Governor sieur de Bienville found New Orleans on the Gulf of Mexico at the mouth of the Mississippi River. French settlements in Louisiana flourish until 1729, when wars with several Indian tribes break out.

A French colonial cottage

•Spanish settlers found the military post and mission of San Antonio in what is now Texas.

1722 The six nations of the Iroquois Confederacy (Mohawk, Oneida, Cayuga, Seneca, and Tuscarora) sign a treaty with the Virginia colonists and agree not to cross the Potomac River or move west of the Blue Ridge Mountains.

AMERICAN HISTORY SOCIETY AND INDUSTRY

1700 The population of the colonies now stands at 275,000.
•French settlers construct fur-trading posts in the Illinois Territory.
•The first commercial rum distillery opens in Boston.

1701 The Reverend Cotton Mather publishes his most popular sermon, *A Christian at His Calling*. In it he argues that salvation demands hard work as well as faith.

1704 French fashions are all the rage in New York. Scarlet stockings and curly wigs for men and long necklaces for women are in great demand.

1709 Quakers in Philadelphia open a center for mental health care, the first of its kind in the colonies.

1712 The New England whaling industry begins when Captain Christopher Hussey captures the first sperm whale off Nantucket Island. Hussey encounters the whale by accident when his ship is driven off course in a storm.
•Pennsylvania bans the importation of slaves.

1713 The first ship of uniquely American design, a schooner, is built at Gloucester, Massachusetts.

1720 The population of the colonies is now estimated at 474,000.

1721 America's first marine and fire insurance company is founded in Philadelphia.

1725 Captain John Jeffrey builds a 700-ton ship at the port of New London, Connecticut.

1725-1749

Jonathan Swift

1726 Irish author Jonathan Swift's novel, *Travels into Several Remote Nations of the World*, popularly known as *Gulliver's Travels*, enjoys instant success.

1730 René Antoine Ferchault de Réaumur, a French scientist, perfects the thermometer.
•Russia and China sign trade agreements and a treaty of friendship.

1737 Swedish botanist Carl von Linné, also known as Linnaeus, publishes his *Genera Plantarum*, introducing an important way of classifying plants and animals.

1740 Frederick II, "the Great," becomes king of Prussia.

1742 Indian slaves in Peru, led by Juan Santos, rebel against the Spanish and defeat them in several battles.

1745 Charles Edward Stuart, "Bonnie Prince Charlie," grandson of James II, arrives in Scotland in an attempt to restore Britain to Stuart rule.
•The War of the Austrian Succession begins when Frederick II of Prussia invades Maria Teresa's Austrian province of Silesia. The Treaty of Aix-la-Chapelle ends the war and returns all lands to Austria except Silesia.

1729 French soldiers in the Louisiana territory massacre Natchez Indians, beginning a ten-year war between the French and the Indians.

1733 James Edward Oglethorpe founds the city of Savannah and the colony of Georgia, the last of the original thirteen English colonies, as a haven for the poor.
•In New York, John Peter Zenger begins publication of the *New York Weekly Journal*. He is appointed the official printer for the colonies of New York and New Jersey after being acquitted of libel in a 1735 trial that established the principle of freedom of the press in the colonies.

The Zenger Trial

1737 Jews are denied the right to vote in New York.

1744 King George's War breaks out in North America between English colonists and French colonists and their Indian allies. New Englanders capture Fort Louisbourg on Cape Breton Island but fail to take Montreal and Quebec. The war ends in 1748 with Fort Louisbourg returned to the French.

1749 Georgia permits large landholdings and slavery, leading to economic prosperity for plantation owners.

1727 Benjamin Franklin forms the Junto, a philosophical club in Philadelphia.

1728 John Bartram of Philadelphia opens the first botanical garden in the colonies.

1731 South Carolina is now exporting 42,000 barrels of rice a year to England.

1733 The "Great Road" is built from Philadelphia to the mouth of the Conestoga River. It makes it easier to bring farm produce to the city.

1734 Canada's population is now estimated at 36,000.

1735 The first colonial medical society is founded in Boston.

1740 Eliza Lucas grows indigo from West Indian seed on her father's South Carolina plantation. The plant, used to produce a blue dye, becomes an important cash crop in the south.
•Benjamin Franklin patents a new kind of stove. It produces more heat for less fuel.

1741 Scottish Protestants from Ireland become the newest wave of American immigrants.

1744 At the top of Boston's bestseller list are *Pamela*, a romantic novel by English author Samuel Richardson, and *The Art of Love* by the Latin poet Ovid.

1747 Virginia settlers and Pennsylvania traders move into the Ohio Territory. French settlers, fearing competition in the fur trade, construct a line of forts across western Pennsylvania.
•The New York Bar Association, the first legal society in the colonies, is founded.

A TIMELINE OF MAJOR EVENTS

1750-1774

WORLD HISTORY

Frederick the Great

1750 Famed composer Johann Sebastian Bach dies in Germany.

1756 Frederick the Great learns of a secret agreement between six European states (including France and Russia) to divide up Prussia between them; the Seven Years' War begins with a Prussian attack on Austria; Britain allies itself with Prussia and declares war on France.
•William Pitt the Elder becomes Britain's secretary of state; his vigorous leadership plays a major role in Britain's rise as a world power.

1757 Robert Clive establishes the rule of the British East India Company over most of India.

1761 Catherine II, "the Great," becomes czarina of Russia.

1762 Britain gains Spanish colonies in the Caribbean and the Philippines.
•France cedes all of its territory west of the Mississippi to Spain.
•Jean-Jacques Rousseau publishes *The Social Contract*, a key text in the philosophical movement called the Enlightenment.

Jean-Jacques Rousseau

1763 The Treaty of Paris ends the Seven Years' War.

AMERICAN HISTORY GOVERNMENT

1753 The Liberty Bell is first rung to call a meeting of the Pennsylvania Assembly; the bell (which cracked during a testing) bears a verse from the Bible: "Proclaim Liberty throughout all the land unto all the inhabitants thereof."

1754 In Albany, New York, Benjamin Franklin proposes that the colonies and the Iroquois Confederacy unite for defense against the French and their Indian allies. The plan is rejected by the colonial legislatures.

A cartoon urging unity

1754 Competing British and French claims to territory from the Appalachians west to the Mississippi lead to the nine years of fighting known as the French and Indian War.

1755 Britain banishes defeated French colonists from Acadia, some of whom travel south to Louisiana, where they become known as Acadians (Cajuns).

1760 The English capture Montreal from the French, essentially ending the war in America.

1773 Parliament passes the Tea Act, giving British merchants a monopoly on the sale of tea to the colonies. In the best-known protest against the Tea Act, Boston Patriots dump tons of tea into the city harbor; similar actions and protests take place throughout the colonies.

AMERICAN HISTORY SOCIETY AND INDUSTRY

1750 German craftspeople in Pennsylvania develop the Conestoga wagon, which becomes the standard vehicle on the frontier.

1750 The colonies' first coal is mined in Virginia.
•Pennsylvanian Jacob Yoder invents the flatboat. It will be used for transporting goods on the Mississippi River.

1751 Sugar is grown and processed for the first time in Louisiana.

1757 Benjamin Franklin designs street lamps for Philadelphia. Whale oil is used as fuel in the lamps.

A sugar mill

1759 The first life insurance company in the colonies, called the Presbyterian Ministers Fund, is organized in Philadelphia.

1762 Ethan Allen establishes a blast furnace and iron works at Salisbury, Connecticut.

1764 John Bartram discovers orange trees growing wild in Florida.

1765 The first chocolate mill in America is built by John Hanna at Dorchester, a town in Massachusetts.

1774 Parliament passes the Coercive Acts in an attempt to crush growing colonial resistance to British rule. The Acts close the port of Boston and reduce the power of the Massachusetts legislature.

1775-1799

1775 Scottish inventor Isaac Watt develops an improved steam engine. Watt's invention encourages the growing Industrial Revolution in England. Watt sells his first steam engine to the industrialist John Wilkinson.

1776 Spain unifies its South American empire by creating the Viceroyalty of Rio de la Plata. It includes Argentina, Bolivia, Paraguay, and Uruguay.

Antoine de Lavoisier

1777 French chemist Antoine Lavoisier proves that air consists mainly of oxygen and nitrogen.

1778 Captain James Cook discovers the Sandwich Islands, later known as Hawaii.

1781 Russia begins construction of the Siberian highway.

1783 In France, the Montgolfier brothers build the first hot air balloon. Their flight lasts ten minutes.

1784 Russia establishes a small settlement on Kodiak Island, Alaska.

1789 In Paris, the French Revolution erupts when a mob captures the Bastille, a fortress prison.

Storming the Bastille

1776 Delegates from twelve of the thirteen colonies meet in Philadelphia. They issue the Declaration of Independence.

1777 Congress authorizes a United States flag, with thirteen stars and stripes.

1778 The Continental Congress approves the Articles of Confederation.

1783 The Treaty of Paris, signed by the United States and Britain, ends the Revolutionary War.

1784 James Madison publishes *Remonstrances Against Religious Assessments*, a pamphlet arguing for the separation of church and state.

1785 Congress passes the Basic Land Ordinance. It establishes the township, an area six miles square, as the basic unit by which new territories are surveyed.

1787 The United States Constitution goes into effect when nine of the thirteen states ratify it.

George Washington

1789 George Washington is inaugurated as the first President of the United States.

1791 Ten amendments to the Constitution are adopted. They are known as the Bill of Rights.
•Vermont becomes the fourteenth state.

1797 John Adams is inaugurated as the second President of the United States.

1775 Benjamin Franklin is chosen as postmaster of the new postal service created by the Continental Congress.

1780 Women ride in the horse races at New York's Hempstead Plains racetrack on Long Island.

1785 Stagecoach lines connect American cities from Boston, Massachusetts, to Savannah, Georgia.
•A mechanized flour mill is invented by Oliver Evans and begins operation in Maryland.

1786 Christopher Collis publishes the nation's first road atlas, *A Survey of the Roads of the United States.*
•Shays's Rebellion, a revolt of poor farmers in Massachusetts who seek tax relief, is put down by the state militia.

1790 The nation's first census determines that the population is 3,929,625, including 697,642 slaves and 59,557 free blacks. Virginia is the most heavily populated state (820,000 inhabitants) and Philadelphia the largest city (42,000 inhabitants).

1792 The nation's first stock exchange is organized in New York City.
•The United States Mint is established in Philadelphia.

1793 The European method of giving houses odd and even numbers on different sides of the street is introduced in Philadelphia.

1795 Boston gets the nation's first tramway. It has wooden rails.

1799 Philadelphia's shoemakers union wins the nation's first organized labor dispute.

Part I

Life and Work on the Colonial Frontier

The first task of America's new settlers was to carve farmlands out of the hardwood forest that once covered eastern North America. Once so dense that a squirrel, it was said, could travel from Maine to the Gulf Coast without touching the ground, this great forest also yielded abundant timber for the building of homes, barns, and fences. This engraving of a farm near Baltimore, still surrounded by virgin forest, first appeared in The Columbian Magazine*, a popular early American publication.*

For more than twenty thousand years North America had been the home of numerous civilizations, of peoples as complex and diverse in their habits and beliefs as the peoples of Europe. Originally crossing the Bering Sea from Asia, generations of migrants had made their way south and east, until they occupied the continent from the Arctic Circle to the Gulf of Mexico and the Atlantic Ocean. And despite their differences, they shared a common knowledge: how to live and survive in harmony with the land.

By the early seventeenth century, as many as half a million Native Americans lived along the eastern seaboard. For the first European settlers, they were a source of invaluable information—and a threat. The first English colony in the Americas, founded on Roanoke Island off the North Carolina shore in 1585, was abandoned, resettled two years later, and mysteriously deserted again. In 1602, eighteen years before the Pilgrims landed on Cape Cod, the first English attempt to colonize the area we now call New England failed. English Captain Bartholomew Gosnold, fearing hostile natives, fled Cuttyhunk Island aboard the *Concord*, taking his crew of eight and a company of adventurers and would-be settlers back to England. Four years later, French explorer Samuel de Champlain charted potential harbors on Cape Cod but was prevented from landing by angry Nauset Indians.

In time, of course, the Atlantic coast was colonized, followed by the slow settlement of the continent's interior. As they became established, the colonists developed ways of life that owed much to their European heritage, and just as much to the challenges and possibilities they found in North America.

THE NATIVE AMERICANS

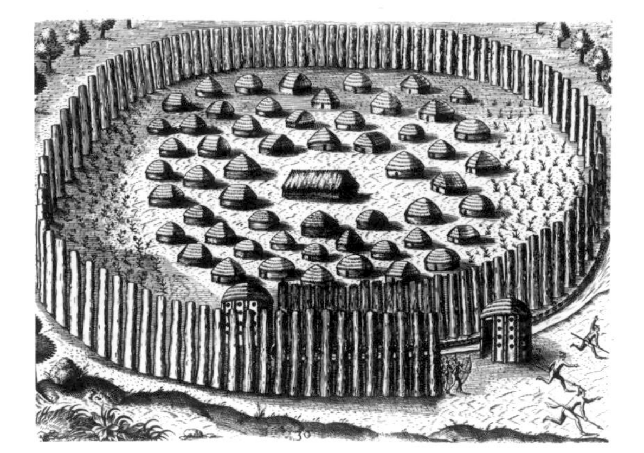

In many ways the social, political, religious, and cultural traditions that European settlers found in the New World were as varied and complex as the ones they had left behind. But instead of cities and written records, the North American Indians preserved oral traditions and nomadic ways of life dating back many thousands of years, even so far as to recall their origins in eastern Asia. Even today, Native American legends about the stars and planets have exact counterparts in Tibetan mythology. When the first white settlers arrived, many North American tribes still preserved the nomadic lifestyle whose slow wanderings had first brought them out of Asia and across the Bering land bridge. But for most Europeans these traditions, and the Indian cultures that sustained them, were difficult to understand. Because they considered the Indians and their traditions un-Christian, most white settlers didn't hesitate to sweep them away when the need arose.

And the need arose often. For although many settlers crossed the Atlantic Ocean in search of religious freedom, many other immigrants were sponsored by companies established to exploit the New World's wealth, by staking a British, Dutch, French, or Spanish claim to this wonderful land and establishing in it the lifestyles of the Old World.

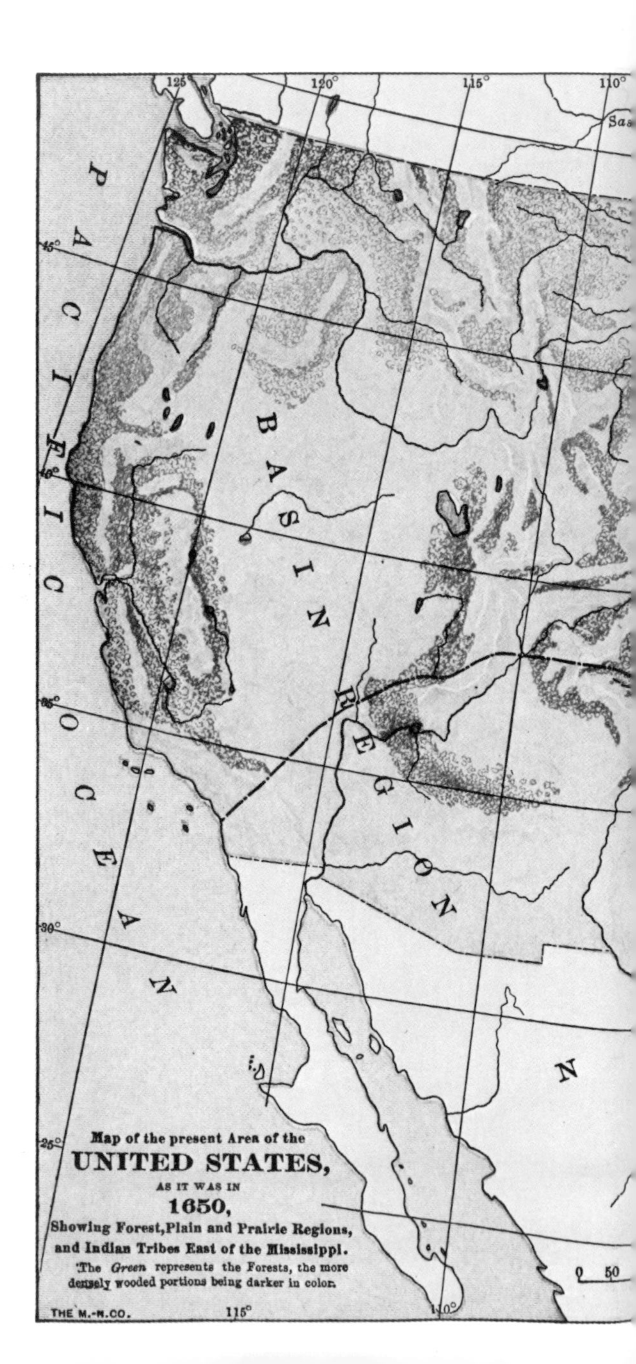

Both colonists and Indians defended their villages. The Timucuas of northern Florida, for instance, circled their homes with a stockade of sturdy logs (left, sketched by French traveler Jacques Le Moyne in 1564). Twice as tall as a man, the stockade had a single, easily defended entrance guarded by lookout posts. Sentinels were said to be able to smell the approach of far-off enemies. To assure their supply of fresh water, the Timucuas often diverted a stream into the village. Their homes, with thatched roofs and walls of loosely woven branches, were grouped around the residence of the village leader or chief.

By 1650, Britain, Spain, Holland, and France had all staked their claims in the New World. In Florida, Spanish settlers vied with native Seminoles and Timucuas. To the north, in what was then called French Florida, French settlers mingled with Creek, Tenassee, and Catawba Indians. From North Carolina to the French settlements of eastern Canada, British and Dutch settlers held sway in lands where coastal tribes and Indians of the Iroquois Confederacy once ruled unchallenged.

A BOUNTIFUL LAND

European settlers learned much about their new land from the American Indians. In particular, the Indians' knowledge of the uses of native plants for food, medicines, and dyes was invaluable to the early homesteaders, who in their own lands had often been craftsmen, not farmers. The settlers also learned the secrets of New World agriculture from the Indians—for example, how to improve the growth and yield of corn by planting a fish-head alongside each plant. They also learned new uses for old materials: How to dress in buckskins, for instance, or turn the bark of the birch tree into a sturdy, lightweight canoe lashed together with the roots of the spruce or white pine.

In return, the Indians gained European trade goods from the new-comers. Guns, knives, axes, and cloth were always popular, and at first the Indians had no objection to sharing their land with the white settlers. But the Indians soon learned that what they were willing to share, the Europeans were determined to own. The Europeans also brought diseases to the New World against which the Indians had no immunity. According to one estimate, the Native American population declined by as much as ninety percent after the Europeans arrived.

Native Americans were highly skilled hunters. This engraving (above), by the Flemish artist Theodore de Bry, after a sketch by Jacques Le Moyne, records the Timucua method of dressing in whole deerskins to stalk their prey. The Timucuas were also excellent mimics of the calls made by the deer they hunted. When they hunted turkeys, the Indians used masks of feathers. In other hunting strategies, Indians used fire to drive their prey out of the forests and into fenced enclosures where they could be killed at leisure or, in the case of buffalo, drove the animals over cliffs to be killed by the fall.

To collect gold carried out of the Appalachian Mountains by rivers, the Indians dug ditches into which the heavy, gold-bearing sand would sink. After collecting the sand, as shown in this engraving by De Bry (opposite, top), the Indians separated the gold it contained and used the gold for ornaments or trade. In Florida, the Timucuas took their gold by canoe down the May River to barter with Spanish traders.

Wherever Native Americans lived, they built boats. This De Bry engraving (opposite, bottom), after a watercolor sketch by John White (who had been a member of the ill-fated Roanoke settlement in 1585), shows how the Secotans, a tribe in Virginia, used fire and scrapers made of shells to fashion a dugout canoe. The engraving also shows how fire was used to fell a tree and remove its branches. Other Native American boats were made of bark or animal skins.

41

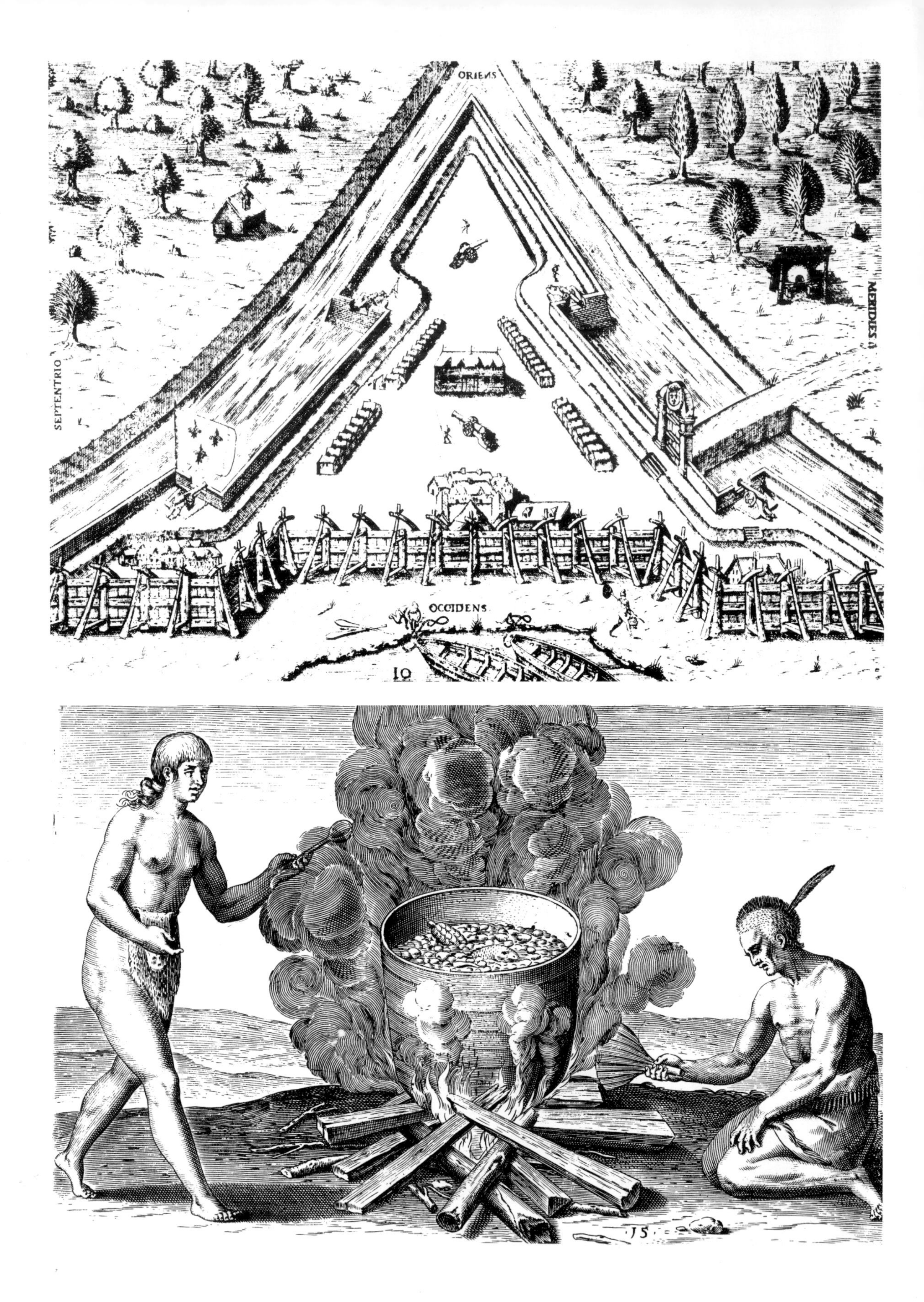
ORIENS
SEPTENTRIO
MERIDIES
OCCIDENS
10
15

The second of two futile attempts by the French to establish trading posts in Florida began in 1563, when René de Laudonnière and four shiploads of French Protestants landed at the mouth of the St. John's River, near present-day Jacksonville, and built Fort Caroline there, shown in this sketch by Jacques Le Moyne (opposite, top) in 1564. Laudonnière returned to France for more supplies, leaving those who remained in Fort Caroline dependent on the Timucua Indians for food. The settlers almost starved to death. Then, in 1565, the Spanish attacked the fort. Although the French surrendered, the Spanish killed most of them and ended French ambitions in the southeast.

Secotan Indians prepared a stew of corn, meat, and fish in a massive earthenware pot (opposite, bottom). Such cooking pots, which were made by the Secotan women, had pointed bases. They were not set upon a fire but were partially buried in the earth for stability, and then a fire was built around them. The English traveler, Thomas Hariot, who observed this scene, believed that even the best English potters could not make vessels to compare with these Secotan pots, and much admired the Secotans' sensible eating habits. American Indians also roasted their food on heated stones or on spits and grills above an open fire.

The English selected the site for the Jamestown colony on May 13, 1607, and settlers arrived in Virginia expecting to make easy fortunes. They were greatly disappointed. On May 26 the settlement was attacked by Indians; within six months 51 of the original 120 colonists had died of disease or famine. Despite these hardships, the Virginia Company continued to advertise the colony (above), claiming that it offered mountains of hidden treasure and an opportunity to meet "very loving Indians."

Before any sort of construction could begin at Jamestown, the swampy island at the mouth of the James River had to be cleared. Then the settlers built a fortified trading post, with thatched, mud-and-wattle houses for the colonists (right).

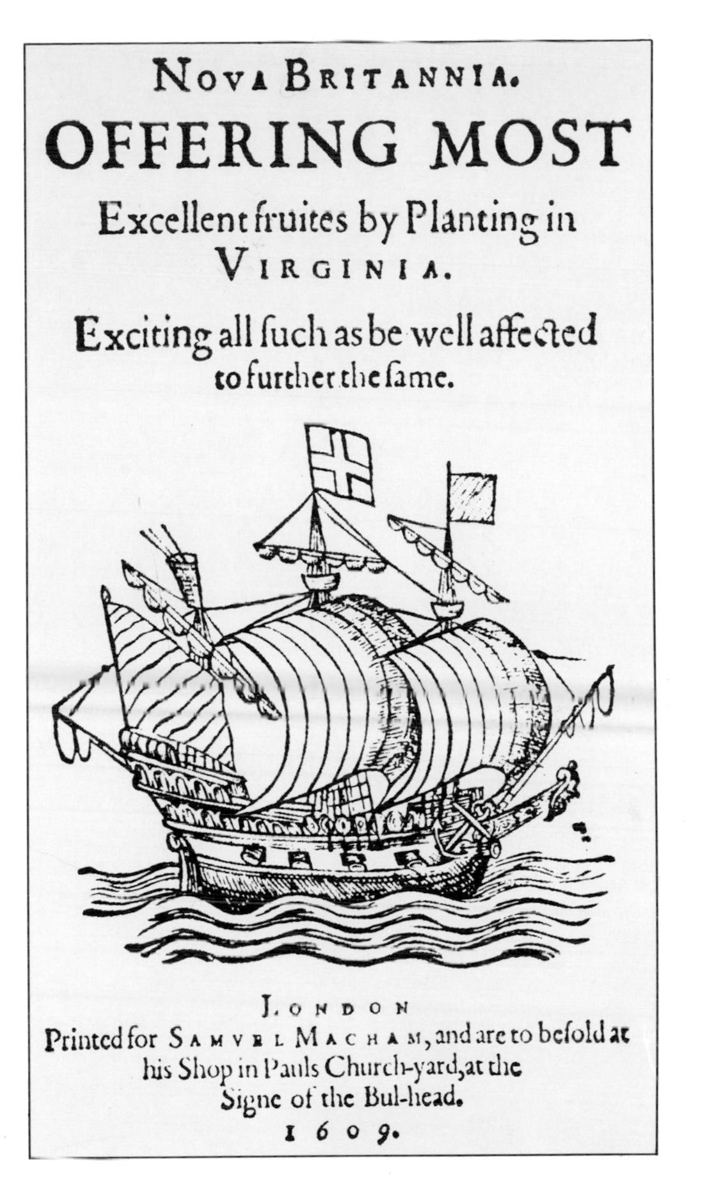

NOVA BRITANNIA.

OFFERING MOST

Excellent fruites by Planting in

VIRGINIA.

Exciting all ſuch as be well affected to further the ſame.

LONDON

Printed for SAMVEL MACHAM, and are to be ſold at his Shop in Pauls Church-yard, at the Signe of the Bul-head.

1609.

THE PILGRIMS AND THE PURITANS

Although the Pilgrims' original goal had been Virginia (their 1620 landfall near what is now Provincetown on Cape Cod was an accident), they were a very different group from the Jamestown colonists. In the first place, their group included families, whereas Jamestown had been settled by single men. Secondly, their motive for leaving England was religious rather than commercial. Thus their mission in the New World had a religious purpose. As the Mayflower Compact, which they signed while still aboard the *Mayflower*, declared, the Pilgrims' journey had been undertaken "for the glory of God and the advancement of the Christian faith, and honour of our King and countrie." To further those ends, the Pilgrims solemnly undertook to "combine ourselves into a civill body politik for our better ordering and preservation," and agreed "to enacte, constitute and frame such just and equall lawes, ordinances, actes, constitutions and offices from time to time, as shall be thought most meete and convenient for the generall good of the Colonie, unto which we promise all due submision and obedience."

In the three and a half months that the Mayflower *was at sea, one man died, and a baby boy named Oceanus Hopkins was born. The cradle in this illustration (left), which appeared in an 1876 issue of* Harper's Weekly *celebrating America's Centennial, rocked the newborn Peregrine White, who was born while the* Mayflower *lay at anchor off Plymouth.*

The Pilgrims probably did not build log cabins, which were later introduced to America by Swedish settlers. But this picture (below), by nineteenth-century artist Howard Pyle, illustrates an important fact: All the colonists shared the work of establishing a new colony.

The Puritans, like their counterparts in England, discouraged fancy dress. In fact, the Massachusetts General Court passed a law in 1634 forbidding such purchases. If a family was wealthy, however, its members often dressed as they pleased. The notion of somber black and brown Puritan apparel, as shown in this woodcut (below) from W. H. Bartlett's The Pilgrim Fathers *(1813) did not actually apply to all colonists.*

By the middle of the seventeenth century, some colonists were secure and established enough to build larger houses for their families. This house (above), also from The Pilgrim Fathers, *is typical of New England architecture. The two floors are built around a large central fireplace. The roof shingles and the clapboard siding were hand-smoothed. At first, oak was used, but pine later became the favored wood. The small windows were made of glass imported from England.*

Only the wealthier colonists brought furniture with them from England. After all, ships were small, and shipping costs high. Wood was plentiful in North America, and artisans were soon turning out furniture. This illustration (right) of a chair made in seventeenth-century New England appeared in the July 15, 1876, issue of Harper's Weekly.

Miles Standish (c. 1564-1656), shown above in a painting by J. E. Baker, leading his men behind an Indian guide, was an English soldier employed by the Pilgrims as their military leader. He saved Plymouth from attack several times and held various posts in the colony. He was one of the founders of Duxbury, Massachusetts, became prosperous in the colony, and helped to buy Plymouth's independence from the London merchants who originally controlled it.

The Puritans stressed the virtues of hard work and time well spent, demanding their children be as industrious as possible in school and around the house. In time these ideals became known as "the Protestant work ethic." This 19th-century woodcut (below) is from a popular reading primer, Thomas Dilworth's A New Guide to the English Tongue.

Family life was perhaps even more important in the colonies than it had been in Europe. Each member had a role to play in the planting and harvesting of crops; in hunting, fishing, and the tending of livestock; and in making clothes and running the house. Survival often depended on cooperation, and a "family" was often an extended affair that included relatives and neighbors (left).

The original settlers at Jamestown were all men. By 1608 there were only two women living in the colony, and it was not until 1619 that a large number of women arrived. Their landing is shown here in a sketch (below) by Howard Pyle that first appeared in Harper's Weekly, *April 1883. The Virginia Company in England recruited unmarried girls to go to Jamestown to improve morale and, it was hoped, increase the colony's population.*

LIFE ON THE FARM

Farming was an occupation for the whole family, and everyone had his or her own tasks. In addition to gardening, women did the cooking, spinning, weaving, and housework. Men and boys were responsible for the heavier jobs—clearing the land, plowing, digging ditches, fencing, and building—and for the hunting expeditions that put fresh meat on the family table. Even young children were kept busy, gathering firewood, shelling peas, and shucking the corn that every farmer grew. Like the Indian farmers, European settlers relied on corn as an easily grown staple. Its grain could be milled for flour and stored as a provision against hard times. Cornstalks were a winter fodder for the cattle, and husks were used to stuff mattresses. Even corncobs had their uses: as stoppers, tool handles, and corncob pipes. On the farm, there were no idle hands, and little went to waste.

Shown here (left) are colonial women farming an onion field, from A General History of Connecticut, *by S. Peters (1829). Women and older girls generally took care of the kitchen gardens, where turnips, onions, peas, and other vegetables were grown.*

This painting (below), by Paul Sandby, is of a settlement farm. An important innovation to the colonial farm, the water mill, can be seen at the left. Mills were used to grind wheat into flour. Running water drove geared wheels and belts to power the mill's machinery.

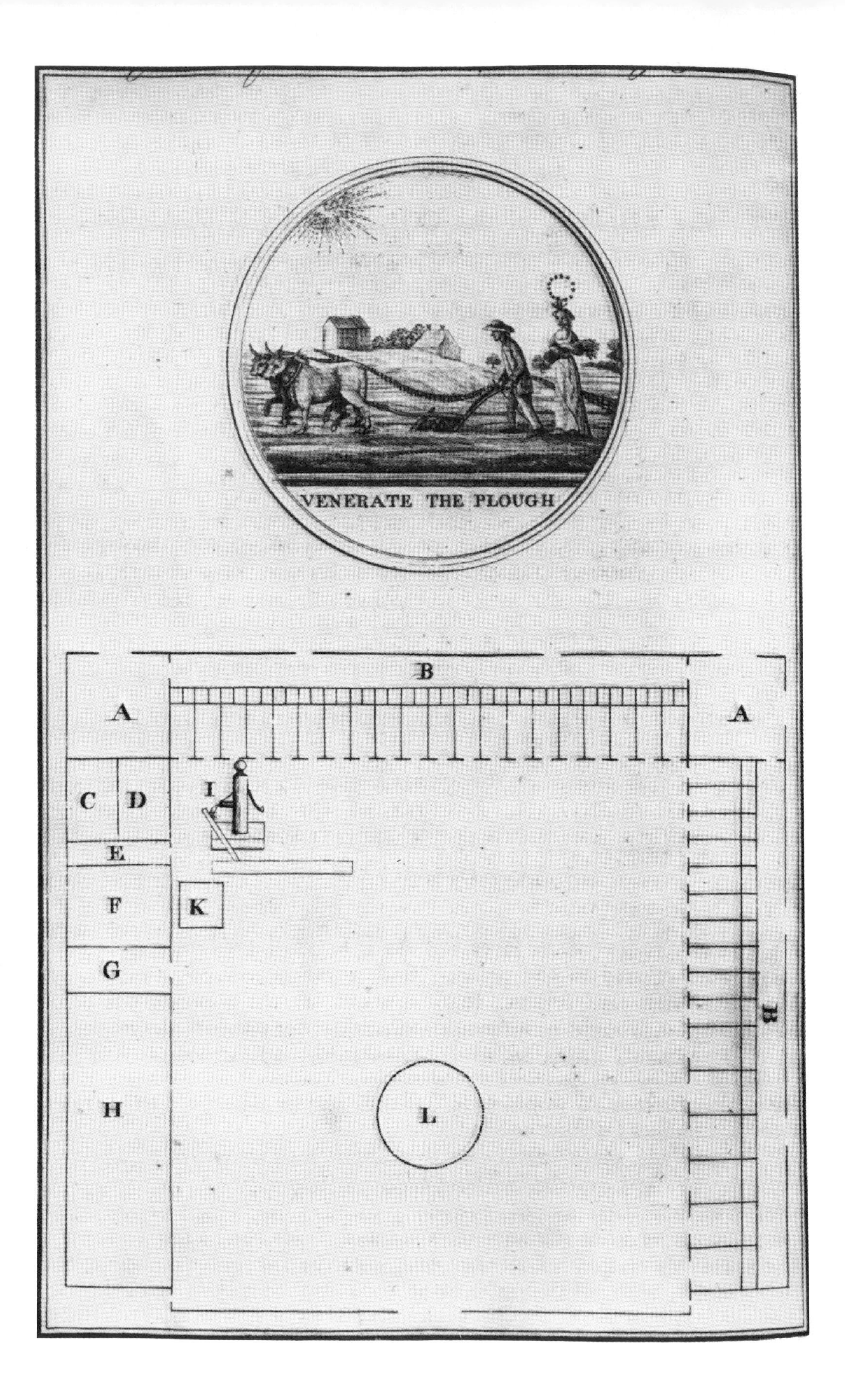
VENERATE THE PLOUGH
B
A
A
C
D
I
E
F
K
G
B
H
L

To tend the Dairy, *and the* Poultry *rear,*
Bake, Brew, *and hive the* Bees *in seasons fair,*
Taught by our Work, the Housewife *learns with ease,*
And while she learns still finds her Stock *increase.*

THE FARMER's WIFE

or

THE COMPLETE

COUNTRY HOUSEWIFE.

CONTAINING

Full and ample DIRECTIONS for the Breeding and Management of TURKIES, FOWLS, GEESE, DUCKS, PIGEONS, &c.
INSTRUCTIONS for fattening HOGS, pickling of PORK, and curing of BACON.
How to make SAUSAGES, HOGS-PUDDINGS, &c.
Full INSTRUCTIONS for making WINES from various Kinds of English Fruits, and from Smyrna Raisins.
The METHOD of making CYDER, PERRY, MEAD, MUM, CHERRY-BRANDY, &c.
DIRECTIONS respecting the DAIRY, containing the best Way of making BUTTER, and likewise *Gloucestershire, Cheshire, Stilton, Sage*, and *Cream* CHEESE.
How to pickle common English FRUITS and VEGETABLES, with other useful Receipts for the Country HOUSE-KEEPER.
Full INSTRUCTIONS how to brew BEER and ALE, of all the various Kinds made in this Kingdom.
Ample DIRECTIONS respecting the Management of BEES, with an Account of the Use of HONEY.

To which is added

The Art of Breeding and Managing SONG BIRDS;
Likewise a Variety of RECEIPTS in COOKERY,
And other Particulars, well worthy the Attention of Women of all Ranks residing in the COUNTRY.

Instructions, full and plain, we give,
To teach the Farmer's Wife,
With Satisfaction, how to live
The happy Country Life.

LONDON,
Printed for ALEX. HOGG, in Pater-noster Row.
(Price One Shilling and Six-pence.)

Farms in the northern colonies were not large, as southern plantations tended to be. This plan of a farmyard (opposite), engraved for Columbian Magazine, *illustrates a compact and efficient use of space. Northern farmers were self-sufficient, growing wheat and corn to feed both family and livestock.*

The Complete Country Housewife *(above) was first published in London around 1770. It was a very popular guide to country living, and many settlers brought it with them from Britain when they moved to the colonies. The book contained instructions for preparing meats, growing and preserving vegetables, and brewing beer and ale.*

SLAVERY AND TOBACCO

Tobacco was just what the colonists needed: a cash crop that could be exported to England and the rest of Europe to pay for imported goods. In the illustration (below) slaves manufacture the barrels in which Virginia tobacco will be shipped to England.

Ships delivering slaves from Africa to America stopped in the West Indies to pick up molasses (from which the colonists distilled rum), delivered their slaves to Newport, Charleston, or another center of the slave trade, and loaded up with tobacco for the return trip to Europe. In this Pyle illustration (right), the first slaves from Africa arrive in Jamestown.

As farms grew larger, which was an especially southern trend, the demand for cheap labor increased. At first it was met by indentured servants from England. In return for their passage to the New World, these servants agreed to work for an American master for a specified period of time. In 1619, though, a new source of cheap labor was found. In that year, the first African slaves were shipped to America. By 1700, slaves accounted for about twenty percent of America's non-Indian population, many of them working the tobacco plantations of Virginia and the Carolinas. And by 1749 George Whitfield, a pioneer Methodist minister, could declare that slaves were "as necessary to the cultivation of Georgia as axes, hoes, or any other utensils of agriculture."

High-grade tobacco had been introduced into Virginia from the West Indies in 1613, three years before slavery reached America, by Captain John Rolfe. He imported seed from the West Indies and crossed the plants grown from it with the local tobacco plants used by the Indians.

Tobacco became a way of life in the colonies where it was grown. For many purposes, it was used in place of money. Warehouse receipts were used like bank checks, and ministers of the Church of England had their salary calculated in pounds of tobacco. In the mid-eighteenth century, when tobacco was worth sixpence a pound, a parson was valued at seventeen thousand pounds a year.

Once the tobacco reached England, it was taxed and then sold on the local market as snuff or pipe tobacco, or re-exported to other European countries. Along with the tobacco shipment, an English tobacco merchant would usually receive a list of goods required by the grower. The merchant would ship these to him, and deduct their price from the grower's credit when his tobacco had been sold. This drawing (right) of tobacco merchants accompanied a map of Virginia and Maryland engraved by Joshua Fry and Peter Jefferson.

Tobacco was planted in April and cut in August. The plants were taken to a shed where they were hung up for drying. The shed had a roof, but its sides were open to permit the tobacco to dry. Tobacco was cured this way for about six weeks, and then "prized" or valued. The cured leaves were then stripped from the plants and packed into hogshead barrels for storage in a public warehouse and official inspection. These steps in the process are drawn in this engraving (below) from Universal Magazine *in 1750.*

Hogsheads of tobacco were four feet high, had a diameter of two-and-a-half feet, and weighed between a thousand and thirteen hundred pounds. From the warehouse they were taken by boat or wagon to a port for shipment to England, as shown here (right) in a print that originally appeared in W. Tatham's An Historical and Practical Essay on the Culture and Commerce of Tobacco, *1800.*

THE SETTLEMENT OF PENNSYLVANIA

When William Penn arrived in America from England in 1682, he already had plans for a new kind of city. Philadelphia was to be "a Greene Countrie towne, which will never be burnt (its houses were all to be of brick), and allways be wholsome." The streets would be spacious and would be laid out according to a tidy and then novel gridiron pattern. Open spaces would be preserved. And, in keeping with Penn's Quaker convictions, the City of Brotherly Love and the province of Pennsylvania would be open-minded. They would be havens for all those who had suffered religious persecution in Europe. In less than one hundred years, Penn's new city would also be the place where America declared its own independence.

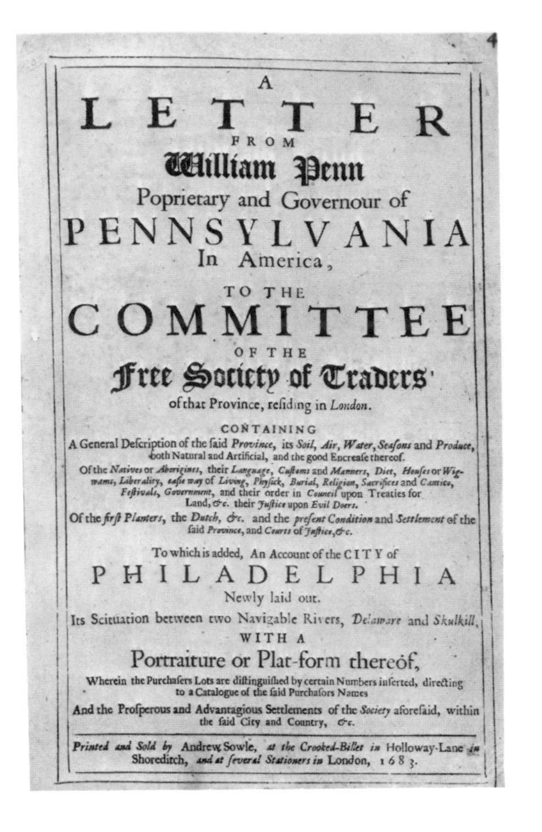

A
LETTER
FROM
William Penn
Popriетary and Governour of
PENNSYLVANIA
In America,
TO THE
COMMITTEE
OF THE
Free Society of Traders
of that Province, residing in *London*.

CONTAINING
A General Description of the said *Province*, its *Soil*, *Air*, *Water*, *Seasons* and *Produce*, both Natural and Artificial, and the good Encrease thereof.
Of the *Natives* or *Aborigines*, their *Language*, *Customs* and *Manners*, *Diet*, *Houses* or *Wigwams*, *Liberality*, *easie way* of *Living*, *Physick*, *Burial*, *Religion*, *Sacrifices* and *Cantico*, *Festivals*, *Government*, and their order in *Council* upon Treaties for Land, &c. their *Justice* upon *Evil Doers*.
Of the *first Planters*, the *Dutch*, &c. and the *present Condition* and *Settlement* of the said *Province*, and *Courts* of *Justice*, &c.

To which is added, An Account of the CITY of
PHILADELPHIA
Newly laid out.
Its Scituation between two Navigable Rivers, *Delaware* and *Skulkill*,
WITH A
Portraiture or Plat-form thereof,
Wherein the Purchasers Lots are distinguished by certain Numbers inserted, directing to a Catalogue of the said Purchasors Names
And the Prosperous and Advantagious Settlements of the *Society* aforesaid, within the said City and Country, &c.

Printed and Sold by Andrew Sowle, *at the Crooked-Billet in* Holloway-Lane *in* Shoreditch, *and at several Stationers in* London, 1683.

William Penn's advertisements for Pennsylvania were unusually candid. A year before he published his Letter to the Committee of the Society of Free Traders (above), he had distributed a tract throughout Europe which guaranteed complete religious freedom and offered land at very reasonable rates.

Settlers in Pennsylvania found lodging in various ways. Here, in a painting by Howard Pyle (below), a family found a cave, dug it out, and raised a roof.

Although Penn had hoped Pennsylvania would become a center for the fur trade (above), that didn't happen. Albany, New York, retained its primacy, and Pennsylvania remained free of the hostilities the trade usually produced between colonists and Native Americans.

Quakers belonged to a religious sect founded in England by George Fox around 1650. They stressed the prime importance of direct, personal communication with God. Believing in the equality of all men and women, they were at odds with the rich and powerful. They saw no need for an ordained clergy, and thus angered established churches. As a result of their beliefs, they were persecuted. In England, they were imprisoned. In America, laws were passed against them in all colonies except Rhode Island and Pennsylvania, and they were whipped, imprisoned, tortured, and hanged. Despite all this, the Quakers flourished and preached in the streets, as shown in this painting titled "A Quaker Exhorter in New England" by Howard Pyle (right).

IMPROVEMENTS IN AGRICULTURE

To survive in their new homeland, America's settlers needed every advantage they could discover or afford. Their fields were stubborn virgin ground, not the soft soil that European farmers had cultivated for hundreds of years, and the trees they cut down were often far more massive than anything in the European forests. In this new environment imported tools were often inefficient, and always expensive.

So the settlers made their own tools, and in doing so improved the traditional designs. The clumsy European axe was replaced by a lighter, better-balanced model with a curved handle. The medieval straight-handled scythe that European farmers still used gained a more efficient curved blade and easily swung handle. Moreover, the fact that the settlers came from many areas, bringing different tools with them, meant that American farmers had a greater variety of tools than their European counterparts.

Buildings, as well as tools, were adapted to the new environment. The barn and threshing-floor were often placed under the same roof as the cow stalls (in England they had been separate buildings), and the whole complex was often connected directly to the farmhouse. In New England's bitter winters, it was a plan that made sense.

Before mowing machines were invented, making hay was a major job for the whole family. When the grass was fully grown, the men cut it with scythes, and the women raked it into piles, or haycocks, using wide rakes with wooden teeth, shown here in an engraving from Diderot's Encyclopédie *(above). Every few days the haycocks would be turned with a pitchfork to help the hay dry evenly. Finally, the dry hay would be built into a haystack (which might even be thatched to keep the rain off), or carted into the barn for winter storage.*

Grain crops—wheat, barley, oats—were cut with a sickle and bound into sheaves with a "rope" of plaited stalks. Six, eight, or twelve sheaves were then arranged in stacks for drying in the field before being taken to the threshing barn. There the sheaves were unfastened, spread on the floor, and beaten with flails to separate the grain from the stalks. Grain and chaff were shoveled up into a winnowing-basket for separation (shown below in another engraving from Diderot's Encyclopédie*). The leftover straw was saved for use as cattle bedding.*

This illustration, from Diderot's Encyclopédie *(above), shows an eighteenth-century dairy. The woman is making butter in a traditional churn (figure 1).*

The several stages of cheese-making are shown in another image (below) from Diderot's Encyclopédie*. Whey is being pressed from the curds, which will then be wrapped in cloth and join the two cheeses already hanging from the rafters for curing.*

The introduction of the ox as field labor helped farmers immensely. As shown in this engraving (this page, top) from the Columbian Magazine*, September 1788, the animal could haul large loads of grain or hay from the fields or pull a heavy plow. Oxen were also more sure-footed and steadier than horses, and were therefore preferred for hauling lumber out of the woods.*

As colonists became financially secure and more settled in their new land, they were able to build larger homes and set them at a distance from their barns and cattle sheds, shown in this engraving (above) of Green Hill Farm near Philadelphia. Fruit trees and gardens for vegetables, herbs, and flowers (to serve the bees that provided many families with honey at a time when sugar was an imported luxury) were often planted around the house. A wealthy family probably had a laundry, summer kitchen, and smokehouse in its yard.

For grain to be kept for long periods, it had to be properly dried and stored in a way that would prevent its becoming musty or mildewed. Granaries like the one pictured here (right), from the Columbian Magazine*, dating from 1779, were designed with several ventilation ports and loading doors; at the bottom was a hopper from which the grain could be easily withdrawn.*

Fig. 1
AIR
A
B
B
C
AIR
D
E
F
G

CLOTH IN THE COLONIES

Although the wealthiest settlers preferred to import their clothes from Europe, most Americans had no choice but to make their own or buy the local product. Flax, from which linen was produced, grew well in the New World, and American sheep produced good wool. Linen and wool, usually dyed with indigo in various shades of blue, were the most popular materials for clothing, and weaving became an important cottage industry. By 1770 a single town, Lancaster, Pennsylvania, was weaving cloth at a rate of 70,000 yards a year. One weaver there, a woman who also ran the town's most genteel public house, singlehandedly produced a hundred yards of cloth a month. Generally, a woman working full-time was expected to produce about six yards a day.

Linen-making was a complex process. In the fall, the flax plants were gathered and left on the ground through winter to rot. This softened the woody outer part of the plant, and made it easier to extract the inner fibers. But extracting the fibers was still a difficult task. It was done by beating the flax with a wooden paddle, or "swingling knife." Then the flax was combed with a long-toothed "hatchel" to separate the tow—the short or broken flax fibers that were used for making twine, ropes, and cheap work clothes—as shown above in an aquatint by W. Hincks.

The long fibers were then wound onto the distaff for spinning on the linen wheel (left). This was about twenty inches in diameter, and was driven by a foot treadle. The finished thread was woven into linen shirts, dresses, sheets, tablecloths, and handkerchiefs; combined with cotton, it produced a durable cloth called fustian.

Sheep-shearing, shown in the top panel of this engraving from Universal Magazine *(opposite page), took place in the spring, relieving the sheep of their heavy winter coats. Once sheared, the fleece was sorted and graded. The finest wool came from the sides of the sheep, while the belly and throat produced a much coarser grade. Other grades of wool were obtained from the back flanks of the sheep. Before the wool could be turned into yarn, it had to be washed (bottom, left) to remove the dirt and excess grease, and then beaten (bottom, right). After it was beaten, the wool was carded or combed to straighten the fibers, then colored, and, finally, dried.*

A.
D
B
C

A NEW ARISTOCRACY IN THE SOUTH

Six of the English colonies were created by King Charles II as land grants to loyal followers. Among them was Carolina, the region between Virginia and the latitude of present-day Daytona Beach in what was then Spanish Florida. The eight men who received the "Carolina Charter," in 1663, had clear ideas about the future of their province: the soil and weather would make it an ideal place to produce exotic, semi-tropical goods—silk, wine, olives, currants—that had been tried in Virginia without success.

To further this dream, the new proprietors devised an exotic Constitution for their vast property. Anyone purchasing 3,000 acres in Carolina would become a Baron; a 12,000-acre purchase would bring the title of Cassique, and those with 20,000 acres would be Landgraves. Ordinary people would be allowed to elect a House of Commons, but none of its bills would become law without consent from a majority of Barons, Cassiques, and Landgraves.

This Constitution, uniquely unsuited to the affairs of a pioneer colony, was largely ignored, and the eventual success of Carolina owed more to rice, tobacco, and immigration by hard-working French Protestants than it did to silkworms, wine, or Cassiques.

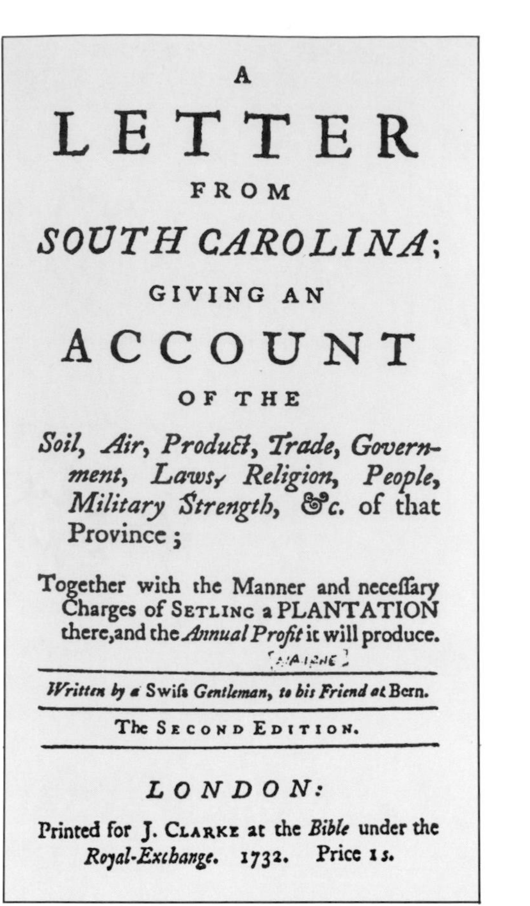

A

LETTER

FROM

SOUTH CAROLINA;

GIVING AN

ACCOUNT

OF THE

Soil, Air, Product, Trade, Government, Laws, Religion, People, Military Strength, &c. of that Province;

Together with the Manner and necessary Charges of SETLING a PLANTATION there, and the *Annual Profit* it will produce.

Written by a Swiss *Gentleman, to his Friend at* Bern.

The SECOND EDITION.

LONDON:

Printed for J. CLARKE at the *Bible* under the *Royal-Exchange*. 1732. Price 1 s.

Although Carolina was chartered in 1663, advertisements for the colony (top), designed to attract new settlers and investors, were still being circulated in Europe fifty years later. To attract people to Carolina, the region's climate and potential for supporting exotic industries was stressed. Workers are weaving silk in this woodcut (above).

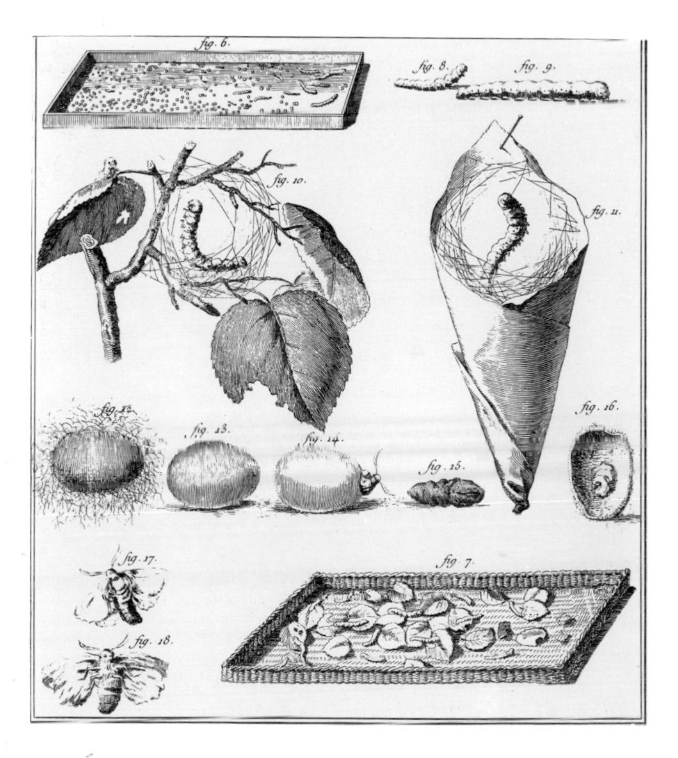

Although there were giant plantations in the southern colonies, ordinary people led lives similar to those in the northern colonies. Small farms and simple houses like the one in this nineteenth-century engraving (top), where Andrew Jackson, seventh president of the United States, was born in 1767, were common.

This diagram, which appeared in Diderot's Encyclopédie, *shows a hatching-tray, on which silkworm eggs hatch into caterpillars, which are then fed on a diet of fresh mulberry leaves. In due course, the silkworm spins its silky cocoon, sometimes on a twig and sometimes in a paper cone provided by the silkworm farmer. After the silk unravels from the cocoon, most chrysalises (figure 15) are killed; those few that are allowed to live (figures 17 and 18) produce eggs for the next generation of worms. Raising silkworms was a skilled and time-consuming job; for southerners, tobacco and rice proved easier and more profitable crops.*

MILLS AND FARMING

As settlements grew to become villages and towns, new businesses and industries developed. Many made use of the most readily available resource, water. A single salt works, for example, could evaporate enough sea water to produce salt, which was widely used as a preservative for meat, as well as for cooking. And a single water-powered mill could serve the needs of farmers for miles around. Now, instead of grinding their own corn or sawing their own lumber, farmers took their grain or wood to the local sawmill or gristmill. Mill operators usually kept part of the grain or lumber as payment and re-sold it, locally or outside the community. Mills and warehouses went together, commerce became more centralized, and what farmers lost in independence they gained in convenience.

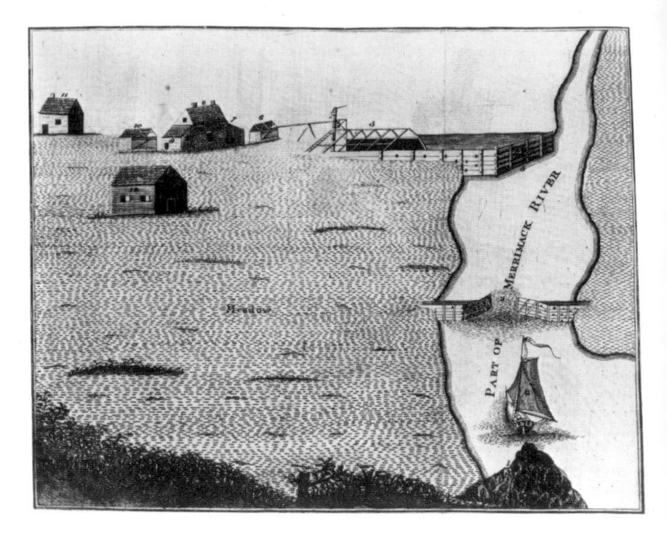

This image (above) of a salt works on the Merrimack River, near Salisbury, Massachusetts, was first published in Pennsylvania Magazine, *March 1776. It took a cord of wood (a stack eight feet long, four feet high, and four feet wide) to boil enough sea water to make eleven bushels of salt.*

The gristmill—one that took grain and made it into flour—made life much easier for farmers. Communities often offered free land to encourage their construction, for building a mill was very expensive. This illustration of a gristmill (opposite, top) appeared in The Young Millwright, *by O. Evans (1795). This particular mill was fully automatic, and required only one operator.*

By harnessing waterpower to turn trees into lumber, the sawmill, such as the one in this engraving (opposite, bottom) from a late eighteenth-century magazine, quickly replaced the sawyer (a person who used a saw manually to make lumber). Two people working in a saw pit could produce about a hundred board-feet of lumber a day; a sawmill could produce that much in an hour or less. By 1700 nearly every town in New England that lay near a stream had a sawmill. A farmer could float cut trees down a stream to the mill and have them turned into lumber to build a bigger house or barn, or the lumber could be shipped to England. Thanks to waterpower, even forests could be exported.

Plate VIII. Art. 89.
Scale of Feet
James Poupard Sculpt

FISHING IN THE COLONIES

On Midsummer Day in 1497, John Cabot and a crew of eighteen aboard the *Matthew* made landfall on the North American coast, perhaps somewhere northeast of Newfoundland. The explorers met no natives but found Indian fishing nets and saw evidence of vast schools of cod. Like Columbus, Cabot had been searching for a western passage to the Orient, and he had hoped to discover not only new territories for the English crown, but gold, silks, and spices as well. Nonetheless, it was the modest codfish, whose firm flesh could be preserved better than that of other fish, that also stimulated European interest in North America. In 1500 the Portuguese sailor Gaspar Côrte-Real rediscovered Newfoundland, and within a few years Portuguese, French, and English vessels were fishing off the Grand Bank and curing their catch on America's northern shores.

With the founding of the Massachusetts Bay Colony in 1630, cod fishing became a firmly established industry and a major trade item. An Englishman, the Reverend Hugh Peter, established the first fisheries at Marblehead. By 1665, about 1,300 fishing boats were working the cod-rich waters of Cape Sable Island at Nova Scotia's southern tip.

This woodcut (above) shows a typical eighteenth-century fishery. Cod were caught on sturdy lines like the one held by the fisherman in the left foreground. Behind him is a three-masted fishing boat and the dock on which its catch was landed. Other stages in the processing of the catch are the cleaning of the fish (figure H), pressing it to obtain cod-liver oil (figures I and L), and drying the pressed fish on a table.

Many colonists found it easier to harvest the sea than to clear the land and make a living with the plow. New Jersey's first permanent white settlement, depicted in this late eighteenth-century watercolor (below), was the coastal village of Horsimus.

The trawling net (above) was more efficient than the line. But for sheer bulk, whales were the favored catch, being greatly in demand for the whale oil that was used for lamps and was a valuable export. Cape Cod, where blackfish are still sometimes beached in large numbers, was the first center of New England's young whaling industry. In the engraving below, a whale has been hauled onto the shore by a windlass; the man on its back is about to strip the blubber with a knife.

LIFE ON THE FRONTIER

The first colonial settlements were coastal, but many pioneers believed their best chances in the New World would be found in the real wilderness to the west, in lands with unknown resources, and no governments to limit enterprise or adventure. For such men and women, rivers formed natural highways through the wilderness. It was by river routes that the first informal explorations of the continent's interior began, creating a steadily westward-moving sequence of new frontiers. In colonial times, the Far West was Ohio. For both pioneers and those who stayed behind in the established regions of the colonies, the image of the frontier was a powerful emblem of New World opportunity and resourcefulness.

George Washington (1732-99; above) began his career by working as a surveyor, shown in this engraving from a nineteenth-century textbook. Washington applied his experience in the frontier later on, when he served as a military leader in the French and Indian War (1754-63).

This map of the Ohio River (opposite, top) was drawn in 1766 by Captain Harry Gordon, who explored the Ohio and Mississippi rivers in order to defend British interests in the west. Rivers were invaluable landmarks for the New World's first surveyors. They were also important in locations where good roads had not yet been built. Western settlers relied on rivers to transport goods between frontier communities and the growing cities of the east.

Pioneer communities of the new west were largely isolated from colonial fashions. They tended to preserve European customs, or invent their own. This engraving (opposite page, bottom), from a late nineteenth-century textbook, shows a wedding on the frontier.

River of Ohio by Capt. Harry Gordon Engr.
Muskingum River 250 Yds wide
Hockhocking R. 60 Yds wide
Little Kanhawa
Creek 10 Yds wide
Rapid
Great Kanhawa R.
Creek 15 yards wide
Sandy River

Part II
Daily Life in the Towns and Cities

Philadelphia was among the first colonial cities to provide social services to its poor. An almshouse, which provided food and shelter for the poor, stood on Spruce Street. (This engraving was published by William Birch in 1799.) The Pennsylvania Hospital for the "relief of the sick poor" was opened in 1751 under the sponsorship of Benjamin Franklin and Dr. Thomas Bond.

Colonial America's few cities were all located along the Atlantic coast, and all had deep-water harbors. These were essential for trade with Europe.

By 1740, Boston, with seventeen thousand people, was the largest city in the colonies. But Boston's location on a narrow spit of land limited its growth, and Philadelphia and New York soon became larger. By 1760 New York had eighteen thousand people and Philadelphia twenty-four thousand. Charleston in South Carolina and Newport in Rhode Island were the fourth and fifth largest cities.

Colonial cities were lively, interesting, and bustling places. Some streets were paved, shops sold a greater variety of goods than were found inland, and newspapers flourished. Philadelphia was one of the first planned cities in North America. It was the first to be laid out in the gridiron pattern that most later cities adopted, and each street was numbered.

Colonial cities also had problems. Fresh water was hard to find, there was no organized garbage removal, and sanitation was primitive. Fires were a constant threat to life and property.

BUSTLING CITIES

In 1670, the population of England's colonies in North America was around 85,000; by 1713, it had reached 386,000 and by 1754 stood at 1.5 million. In the same period the land area settled by Europeans tripled.

As part of America's rapidly increasing population pressed westward to settle new frontiers, new cities were established along the eastern seaboard. Norfolk, Virginia, became an outlet for North Carolina's lumber. Baltimore, founded in 1730, flourished by exporting grain from Maryland and Pennsylvania. And as port cities began to compete with each other, they tried to improve their connection with the frontier settlement. In 1733, for example, Philadelphia was spurred by Baltimore's success and built the "Great Road" to the mouth of the Conestoga River. To help bring farm products to the city, the Conestoga wagon was developed.

With the growing wealth of America's cities came schools, colleges, newspapers, and printing presses. New professions arose and a brand new upper class of citizens were becoming rich on trade.

As the English colonies of the north grew in strength, so did the Spanish presence in Florida, though not as quickly. St. Augustine, founded as a Spanish fort in 1565, is the oldest continuously inhabited city in the United States. This street scene (above) reflects the Spanish heritage of its buildings and fashions.

By 1740, as this map (opposite page) shows, European colonists had settled large parts of eastern North America as far west as the Appalachian Mountains. In New York, western expansion was slowed by the strength of the Iroquois Confederacy, and by the large land grants made in the seventeenth century to the Patroons (owners of huge estates) of the Hudson River valley. In the Southeast, except for communities like Augusta and Camden on the Savannah and Santee rivers, settlement was still largely confined to the Atlantic coast and its many rivers—an area often called the Tidewater.

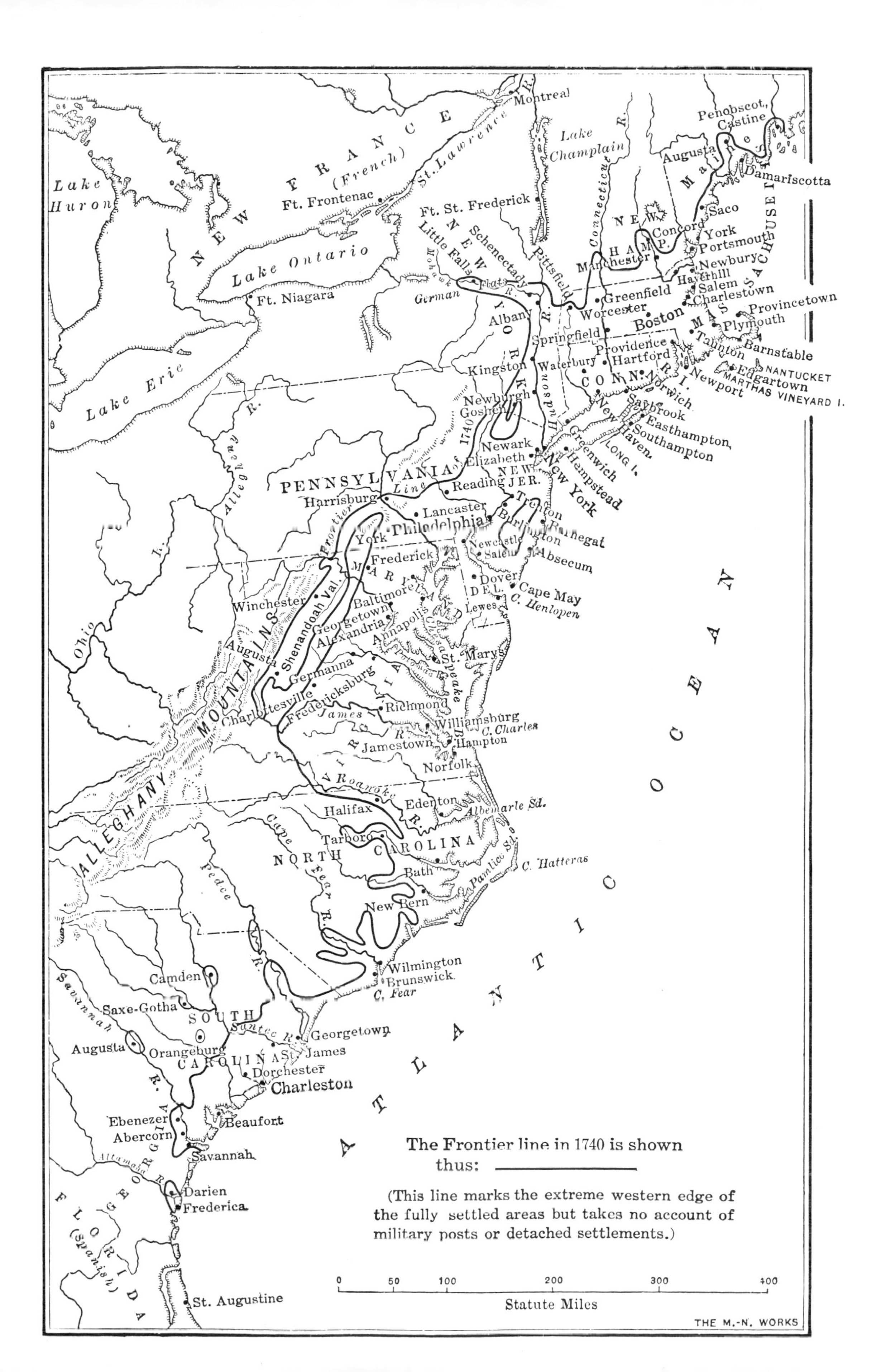
NEW FRANCE (French)
Montreal
Lake Huron
Lake Ontario
Lake Erie
Lake Champlain
St. Lawrence
Ft. Frontenac
Ft. Niagara
Ft. St. Frederick
NEW YORK
Schenectady
Little Falls
Albany
Kingston
Newburgh
Goshen
German Flats
Pittsfield
Connecticut R.
Hudson R.
NEW HAMP.
Concord
Manchester
Maine
Penobscot, Castine
Augusta
Damariscotta
Saco
York
Portsmouth
Newbury
Haverhill
Salem
Charlestown
Boston
MASSACHUSETTS
Provincetown
Plymouth
Barnstable
Taunton
Greenfield
Worcester
Springfield
Providence
Hartford
Waterbury
CONN.
R.I.
Newport
Norwich
NANTUCKET
Edgartown
MARTHAS VINEYARD I.
Saybrook
New Haven
Easthampton
Southampton
LONG I.
Greenwich
Hempstead
New York
Newark
Elizabeth
NEW JER.
Trenton
Burlington
Barnegat
Absecum
Cape May
PENNSYLVANIA
Line of 1740
Frontier
Harrisburg
Reading
Lancaster
Philadelphia
York
Newcastle
Salem
Dover
DEL.
Lewes
C. Henlopen
Frederick
MARYLAND
Baltimore
Georgetown
Alexandria
Annapolis
St. Marys
Chesapeake B.
Potomac R.
Winchester
Shenandoah Val.
Augusta
Germanna
Charlottesville
Fredericksburg
VIRGINIA
James R.
Richmond
Williamsburg
C. Charles
Jamestown
Hampton
Norfolk
Roanoke R.
Edenton
Albemarle Sd.
Halifax
Tarboro
NORTH CAROLINA
Bath
Pamlico Sd.
C. Hatteras
New Bern
Cape Fear R.
Wilmington
Brunswick
C. Fear
Pedee R.
Camden
Saxe-Gotha
SOUTH CAROLINA
Santee R.
Georgetown
Orangeburg
St. James
Dorchester
Charleston
Augusta
Savannah R.
Ebenezer
Abercorn
Beaufort
Savannah
GEORGIA
Altamaha R.
Darien
Frederica
FLORIDA (Spanish)
St. Augustine
ALLEGHANY MOUNTAINS
Allegheny R.
Ohio
ATLANTIC OCEAN
The Frontier line in 1740 is shown thus:
(This line marks the extreme western edge of the fully settled areas but takes no account of military posts or detached settlements.)
0 50 100 200 300 400
Statute Miles
THE M.-N. WORKS

SEATS OF GOVERNMENT AND COMMERCE

In the first half of the eighteenth century the cities of the mid-Atlantic colonies grew rapidly in economic, cultural, and political importance. Two such cities were Williamsburg, Virginia, and Baltimore, Maryland.

Williamsburg, originally known as the Middle Plantation because of its location between the York and James rivers, was settled in 1632 and chosen as Virginia's capital in 1699. It was surveyed and laid out by Theodorick Bland. Its main street was almost a mile long and named for the Duke of Gloucester. To the west, it was bounded by the College of William and Mary, and to the east by the Capitol. Thomas Jefferson was an alumnus of the college, and George Washington served as its chancellor for eleven years. From 1704-80 the Capitol was the home of Virginia's House of Burgesses, which unanimously adopted a resolution for American independence there on May 15, 1776. Besides politicians, plantation owners, and students, Williamsburg attracted fine architects and craftsmen, and the city became a showplace of colonial America.

Baltimore owed its growth not to politics but to business, a location on the Patapsco River near Chesapeake Bay, and an excellent natural harbor. The more grain and tobacco America's farmers and plantation owners produced, the more they needed a convenient port for shipping their goods. Baltimore grew rich serving that need.

Settled in the seventeenth century but not incorporated until 1745, Baltimore, shown in this 1752 sketch (below), became a major port and shipbuilding center. Unlike Williamsburg, which lost its position as Virginia's capital to Richmond, Baltimore's growth and importance continued.

Williamsburg's oldest public buildings are pictured in this engraving (above), known as the Bodleian Plate because it was found in the Bodleian Library in Oxford University in 1929. The new statehouse was completed in 1705. The following year its architect, Henry Cary, began work on the elegant Governor's Palace, completed in 1720. The College of William and Mary was founded in 1693. Its central building, probably designed by Sir Christopher Wren, is the one of the oldest academic buildings in the United States.

Bethlehem, Pennsylvania (above), was settled by Moravians, members of a Protestant sect that had suffered persecution in Europe. Both George Washington and Benjamin Franklin admired the Moravians' talent for hard work and self-sufficiency. Industries of all kinds, from wagon making to hat making, flourished in their settlement, along with neat gardens, well-tended pastures, and fruitful orchards.

There was a great demand for glass in the colonies, especially for window panes, bottles, and lamps. In this illustration from a 1747 issue of British Universal *magazine (below, left), a glassmaker, or "gaffer" (center), blows into a blob of molten glass at the end of his blowpipe. At left and right other glassmakers shape their hot glass by rolling it on a block or manipulating it with iron tongues.*

Moravian potters, depicted in this engraving from Diderot's Encyclopédie *(below, right), supplied their customers with all kinds of glazed earthenware, from clay pipes to baking dishes and platters. Some said their work was so fine it resembled expensive imported porcelain.*

Until reorganized by Ben Franklin in 1775, the colonial postal service was expensive and inefficient. Postmen carried mail and only collected payment on delivery. Deliveries were infrequent, and if the postrider didn't have enough mail to make his trip worthwhile, the delivery was canceled. In this 1734 woodcut (above, left), a post rider blows a horn to announce his arrival in a colonial town.

Outside the cities, peddlers served as mobile hardware stores, selling pots, pans, and other household necessities from door to door, as shown in this nineteenth-century woodcut (above, right).

The colonies had no large deposits of tin, so tinsmiths had to buy their raw material from England. From it they made kitchen utensils that were popular because they weighed less than iron and, with their shiny surfaces, were more decorative. In this illustration (below), the smiths are making coffeepots. On the bench, another worker files the rim of the pot to ensure a tight-fitting lid, and the master tinsmith solders the spouts in place.

NEW AMSTERDAM BECOMES NEW YORK

In 1609, the English explorer Henry Hudson, employed by the Dutch, sailed up the river now named for him as far as the rapids north of present-day Albany. In 1624, the Dutch West India Company founded a trading post at Fort Orange (Albany). Two years later the Company purchased the island of Manhattan from local Indians and established the New Amsterdam trading post there. By 1630 the settlement had around three hundred citizens and a busy harbor. Beyond the wall at Wall Street, which was built to keep out Indians and wolves, were "bouweries," or farms.

In 1664 King Charles II of England granted a vast tract of North America, stretching from Maine to the Delaware River, to his brother, the Duke of York. He then declared war on the Dutch. On August 18, 1664, the Duke of York's deputy governor, Richard Nicolls, sailed into New Amsterdam harbor and demanded that the governor, Peter Stuyvesant, surrender to him. After failing to convince the settlers to resist the English fleet, Stuyvesant surrendered without firing a shot. By October the Dutch trading posts had all been captured and New Amsterdam had become New York.

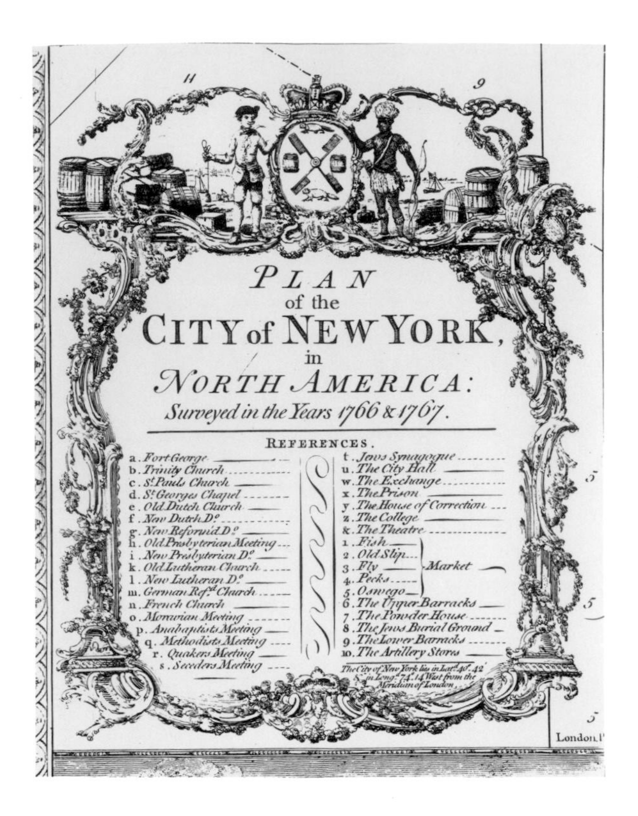

This survey (above) of the City of New York was made in 1767, just over a hundred years after New York had become an English settlement. Published in 1776, it showed how the city had prospered under English rule. Among the sites it plotted were eighteen churches (including a synagogue and several Quaker, Moravian, Anabaptist, and other meeting halls), five markets, a college, a theater, two prisons, several military compounds, and civic and commercial buildings. The survey also showed (below) how far the original settlement had spread beyond the island of Manhattan.

New Amsterdam owed its prosperity to a fine harbor and the access provided by the Hudson River to the fur- and timber-rich regions to the north. In this illustration (right), by nineteenth-century artist Howard Pyle, several Dutch merchants are meeting along the waterfront.

The Dutch also built a canal across the island of Manhattan, connecting the Hudson and the East River. The canal was later filled in. But the city preserved many of its Dutch buildings, as shown in this late-eighteenth-century engraving (below), and continued to grow.

PHILADELPHIA

By 1764, prosperous Philadelphia was the most modern and thoroughly urban city in the colonies. Its population (which the 1760 census recorded as 18,766) enjoyed paved streets, with sidewalks that were lit at night by whale-oil lamps and patrolled by police. The city also had large public buildings, like Carpenter's Hall, later Independence Hall, where the Declaration of Independence was signed, and Christ Church, one of the first American Episcopal churches. Private mansions included Stenton Mansion, built in 1731 by William Penn's secretary, James Logan (which served as headquarters for both George Washington and British general William Howe during the Revolutionary War), and Cliveden, built between 1763 and 1767 for Pennsylvania's Chief Justice, Benjamin Crew. The city also had libraries, three newspapers (one of which was published in German), the only hospital in North America, the first American botanical garden (on the estate of the naturalist John Bartram), a post office run by Ben Franklin, and several markets, including the New Market.

City life freed women from some of the hard work previously done by them on the farm. No longer obliged to weave or weed and tend the kitchen gardens, they spent their time, reading, writing, or taking care of the household. A woman cooks over a hearth in this illustration from Wercken, *a Dutch book about work by Jacob Cats (opposite page, top left).*

People in colonial cities spent much of their day shopping in the new markets that brought country produce into the heart of the city, as shown in this illustration (opposite page, top right), also from Wercken.

This picture (opposite page, bottom), titled "The Country Market Place, Philadelphia," was engraved by William Birch and Sons in 1799. It shows a popular street for shopping in the center of Philadelphia.

LEISURE AND RECREATION IN THE COLONIES

It may seem that the colonists did not have much time for fun, but as hard as they had to work, they made time for play. Even the industrious Puritans developed forms of entertainment. Helping a neighbor build a barn gave rise to the social, and uniquely American, barn raising. Other kinds of community entertainment included cornhuskings and quilting bees. Children in the northern colonies went ice skating and sledding during the winter.

Horse racing was popular all over the colonies. Boston, New York, and Philadelphia all had racetracks. Favorite horses for racing differed with the region. The quarter horse, an American breed adapted to sprinting, was said to have begun with horses bred to race the quarter-mile stretch between Virginia Governor Berkeley's plantation, Greenspring, and Jamestown. The governor and his friends would race the quarter mile every Sunday after church. Other popular pastimes included hunting (all kinds of animals) and cockfighting.

The Puritans were deeply opposed to men and women dancing together, regarding it as "profane and promiscuous." They were also opposed to May Day celebrations and dances around a maypole (top), which they saw as unchristian.

In the southern colonies, though, people looked upon dancing as a pleasant social activity, and a skilled dance teacher could make a good living. For those unable to afford his services, dance manuals (above) were published, with diagrammed instructions.

Hempstead, on Long Island, shown in this nineteenth-century engraving (top), had a fine racecourse. The track was sixteen miles long and four miles wide, and annual horse races were held there as early as 1670. The prize was a silver cup. In 1750, English thoroughbreds were brought to the colonies. With far more endurance than the home-bred horses, these thoroughbreds revolutionized American racing, and most famous American race-horses are descended from them. They made horseracing into a sport for the rich, and left common people to such sports as boules (right, middle), a game similar to lawn-bowling, or billiards (right), a popular game in taverns.

ON THE ROAD

The earliest settlers were usually too busy to travel much. In any case, the settlements were scattered at great distances along the coast. As the number of settlements increased, however, more people began to travel, on foot if they had to, by horse if they were lucky.

At first, roads did not exist. Travelers could try to follow blazed trails, but these were often confusing because they crisscrossed one another. It was easy to get lost. There were few inns, and those a traveler might find were usually dirty and uncomfortable. A better proposition, if the traveler was lucky, was a friendly farmhouse. Often, a lonely farmer's family was glad to feed and house a traveler in return for conversation and news of the wide world.

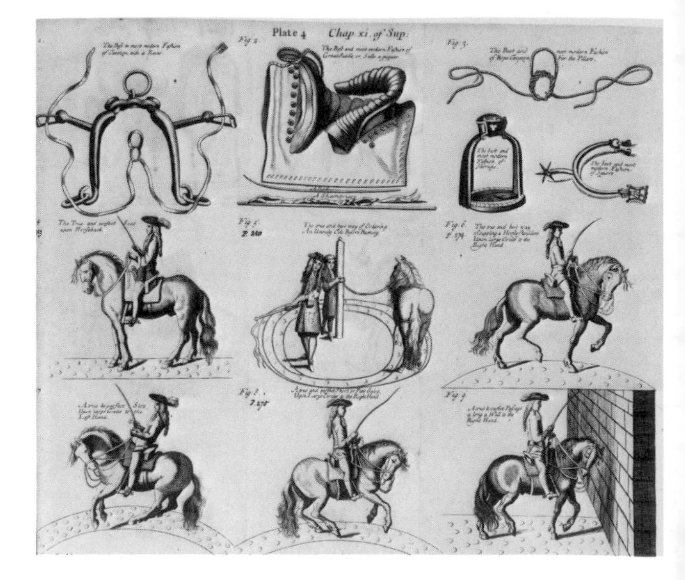

As roads were built through the colonies, the business of the coach maker and harness maker began to grow. Coaches became status symbols, much as automobiles are today. These harnesses (above) appeared in an eighteenth-century book on equestrian equipment.

The chaise (left) was a type of carrriage popular with well-to-do colonists in the eighteenth century. These two-wheel carriages, usually equipped for only one horse, were used more often for pleasure rides than for traveling long distances.

Blacksmiths made and repaired metal goods for their customers. They also shoed horses, as illustrated here in Diderot's Encyclopédie *(above). In the background, a horse is confined in a special frame while its hooves are trimmed.*

In this plate (below), also from Diderot, "joiners"—skilled woodworkers—are crafting a coach model called a berlin.

CRAFTS AND TRADES

The American colonists stressed the dignity of labor, and those who made things with their hands—"mechanicks," as they were called—were essential to the new communities. Thus, craftspeople in the colonies had a different and more respected role than in Europe. They did not, for example, occupy a single class in colonial society. Craftspeople could be found at every level of society, from the wealthy to indentured servants and slaves. This was especially true in the cities. In Philadelphia, for instance, craftsmen, particularly Quakers, often had a high social rank. The records of the Carpenters' Company contain the names of some of the leading figures in Philadelphia society, and the silversmith Philip Syng was elected Treasurer of the American Philosophical Society.

Many craftspeople in Philadelphia, Boston, and Newport, after succeeding as house builders, coach builders, silversmiths, or makers of scientific instruments, went on to become traders and merchants, and entered fashionable society by that route.

A view of Boston (below), made in 1776, shows in its foreground a group of "mechanicks" at work on a variety of tasks. In the middle ground of the picture, land is rolled and plowed, and a stagecoach makes its way out of the city; in the bay are two large sailing ships. The artist incorporates in a single scene all those factors that made Boston a great city: sea trade, agriculture, and the work of skilled craftsmen.

As they had in Europe since the Middle Ages, craftsmen in the colonies formed guilds that were the forerunners of modern trade unions. Among the earliest were the guilds formed by coopers, who made barrels, and printers. This advertisement (right) summons New York's "mechanicks" to an important meeting.

New-York, May 11, 1774.

THE MECHANICKS of this city are requeſted to meet, this evening, at 7 o'clock, at the houſe of David Philipſe, in Horſe and Cart ſtreet, on buſineſs of the utmoſt importance.

This Diderot plate (above) shows house builders at work. Thanks to newly developed sawmills, homebuilders were able to order lumber accurately cut to the dimensions they needed. In the background of the picture is a stack of beams and rafters from the sawmill.

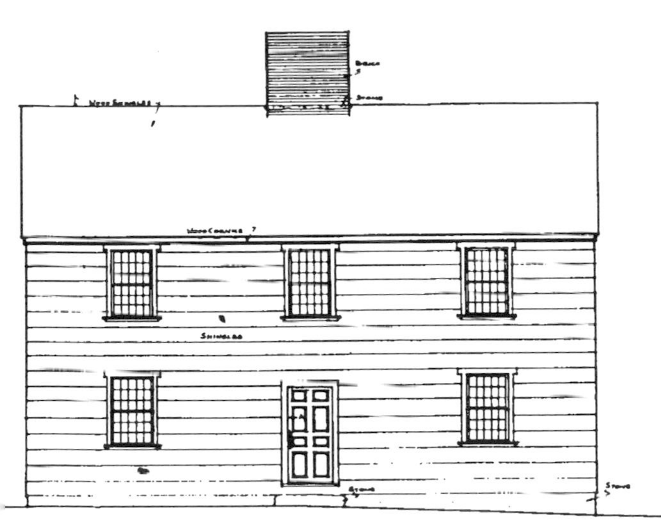

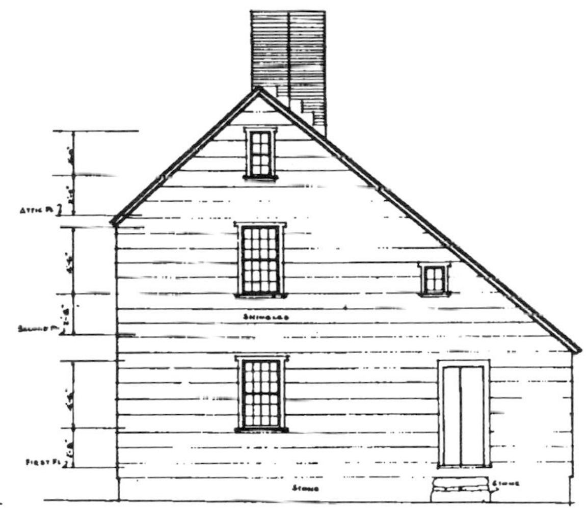

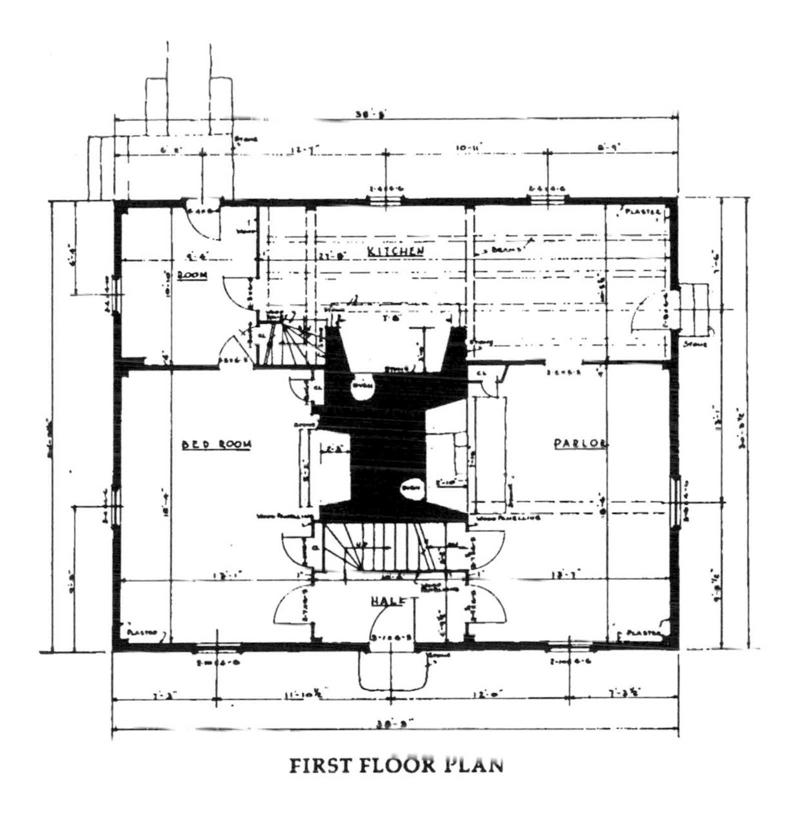

FIRST FLOOR PLAN

The Old Ogden House (top) in Fairfield, Connecticut, dates from 1700 and follows the classic New England design. Like most New England homes, it was built of wood, with a massive, centrally located masonry fireplace and windows with twelve panes in each sash. The floor plan (above) shows the length and width of rafters and uprights and the size of rooms.

THE UPPER CLASSES

Every city had its aristocrats, those citizens whose social position was due to family and wealth. As in Europe, wealth was usually gained by inheritance or trade or from landholdings. Family status came either from a person's European heritage, or from being descended from notable early colonists. The lives of the wealthy closely resembled those of the English gentry. Having both leisure and money, they could afford to spend a morning with the tailor, an afternoon with the cobbler, and an evening at a tavern, a musical entertainment, a dinner, or a ball. They were the customers of the silversmiths and dance masters, the collectors of books, the patrons of colleges and artists.

Cobblers took tanned leather and turned it into shoes, often custom-made for their clients. By 1767, New England's shoemakers were producing eighty thousand pairs of shoes a year, and selling them not only in New England but as far south as New York and Philadelphia. A wealthy customer is fitted with a pair of handmade shoes in this illustration from Diderot's Encyclopédie *(bottom).*

Although a person's clothing was perhaps less important in the colonies than in Europe, it was still the distinct mark of social class, and the wealthy were inclined to wear the richest finery they could afford. Fashions were imported from England and France, either directly or in copies made by skilled colonial tailors. In Philadelphia, master tailors had their own guild, the Taylors' Company, and with their apprentices and journeymen accounted for about fourteen percent of the city's artisans. Customers inspect the range of fabrics at an exclusive tailor's shop in this plate, also from Diderot.

Faneuil Hall in Boston (top) was donated to the city by Peter F. Faneuil as a market and meeting place. Faneuil had made his money through trade with the West Indies. Like him, many rich merchants performed acts of good works to express their civic pride and, incidentally, to improve their social status.

Boston's Green Dragon Tavern (above) was a favorite meeting place for male Bostonians; like all taverns, it was strictly out-of-bounds to women.

EUROPEAN FASHIONS

Port cities were not only centers for the export of American goods to England and the rest of Europe. They were also points of entry for European news, products, ideas, and styles. Americans were eager to hear what was going on in the Old World, and many had the time and money to pay attention to the latest European fashions and designs for everything from furniture to fabrics. They sent away for books and catalogues, and even ordered the harness for their carriage horses from London to be certain that they traveled in the best possible style. In turn, Europeans were fascinated by the New World. But what they craved had little to do with colonial cities or fashions. The American frontier was what interested them, and stories of Indians and pioneer adventures, and pictures of strange plants, animals, and exotic landscapes found an enthusiastic market.

Fashion was less important on the farm than in cities and towns. A woman uses a bowl to cut her husband's hair in this woodcut (opposite, left), as other family members wait their turn.

While country folk got home-style haircuts, city people were interested in high styles. This towering hairpiece and plumed hat with beads and bouquet (opposite, right) was a popular style for women of fashion in the seventeenth century.

Philadelphia's citizens looked forward to a ship's docking to learn of the latest goings-on in Europe (opposite, bottom), and to receive fabrics, books, and other articles ordered months before.

Because colonial settlers came from all over Europe, news from all parts of Europe interested them. This 1877 illustration (below) shows a parade of the Dutch fashions of the eighteenth century.

TRADE AND SHIPPING

Every port supported shipbuilders who produced vessels for the transatlantic and Caribbean trade routes, as well as smaller boats for working local waters. Boston, and New England in general, had a thriving shipbuilding industry; Fishing and whaling fleets provided steady, year-round work and the near-by northern forests provided ample timber. Between 1769 and 1771 Massachusetts shipyards accounted for thirty-five percent of the tonnage of ships built in the colonies, New Hampshire for seventeen percent, and Rhode Island for eight percent. Baltimore's shipyards also became famous for their innovative ship designs.

Many skilled craftsmen—"above 30 Denominations of Tradesmen and Artificers," according to a Bostonian writing in 1749—were involved in completing a new ship. Carpenters and joiners worked on the hulls and masts, ropemakers on the rigging, and sailmakers sewed the sails. Goods were usually carried in barrels, so coopers were always busy. Blacksmiths fashioned nails and other hardware for the ship, but timbers were usually fastened together with wooden pegs called "treenails" or "trunnels."

Shipyards were busy places. When there were no new ships to be built, older ones were always ready to be repaired or refitted.

Navigation was always hazardous in coastal waters. A sloop towing a longboat passes the Boston light (top).Other lighthouses dotted the eastern seaboard, from Maine to the Carolinas. The light of their whale-oil-burning lamps was intensified by a system of mirrors and lenses, and could often be seen for miles out to sea. Each lighthouse flashed its own signal.

Once a ship identified a light, it could gauge its position and judge the whereabouts of hazards and navigable channels. At night and in bad weather, lighthouse beacons were an invaluable aid. This 1780 engraving (above) shows the lighthouse at Cape Henlopen, Maryland

On average it took a year, from keel-laying to launching, to complete a ship, and hundreds of men were employed in the process. The engraving above, of a Philadelphia dock, gives an idea of the scale of the undertaking. In general, colonial shipyards built two kinds of vessels: topsailers and sloops and schooners.

Every city with a shipyard had at least one rope maker's shop (below). One of the largest in the colonies was John Daniel's Boston ropewalk, which could manufacture ropes up to a hundred fathoms (six hundred feet) long, as well as every other type of cord and twine.

PRINTING AND PUBLISHING

Printing began early in the colonies when Stephen Daye began operating a press in Cambridge, Massachusetts, in 1639. A year later he published Cotton Mather's *The Whole Book of Psalmes* —the first book published in English in the New World. A press of the kind Daye used is shown below.

Printing did not make much headway in the early colonies. Presses were expensive and costly to import. By 1700, however, Boston had about a dozen or so presses. Germantown, Pennsylvania, was home to the first German printer and publisher, Christopher Sower. In 1738, Sower published a German-language newspaper. He was also responsible for the first Bible printed in a European language in the New World, in 1743.

Another notable printer of the period was Isaiah Thomas, who published the *Massachusetts Spy* — an influential paper of its time. Thomas later wrote and published the two-volume *History of Printing in America*.

Benjamin Franklin (above) is by far the most notable of the early American printers and publishers. He learned his trade from his brother, who was publisher of The New England Courant. *Benjamin Franklin also worked in Philadelphia and England for printers. By 1729 he published* The Pennsylvania Gazette *in Philadelphia.* Poor Richard's Almanack *established Franklin's reputation. First published in 1732, it continued for twenty-five years. It sold an average ten thousand copies a year—the most widely circulated periodical of its time. As well as being a printer and publisher, Ben Franklin was one of the most notable scholars, authors, scientists, and statesmen of his time.*

This machine (left) is typical of the kind of printing press found in the colonies during the eighteenth century. Type was set in boxes known as cases, inked, and then pressed against paper by screwing down the upright frame.

Advertising cards (above) were a popular way to get the public's attention. This one was put out by one of Boston's many printers. Below, left: A page from the Rhode Island Almanack, published by James Franklin (Ben's elder brother). He established the first press in Rhode Island in 1727. Below, right: The title page of one of Benjamin Franklin's many books, a collection of Pennsylvania laws and charters that he published in 1740.

NOVEMBER. *XI Month, hath* XXX *Days.*

D. H.			
Full	●	3	4 mor.
Laſt	Q.	10	midnight
New	☽	17	5 mor.
Firſt	Q.	25	8 mor.

☊ { 1 27 / 11 ♐ 27 / 21 26 } Deg.

Planets Places. D.	☉	♄	♃	♂	♀	☿	☽'s Lat.	
	♏	♌	♐	♋	♐	♎		
1	9	16	23	1	26	25	N.	3
6	14	17	24	1	♑ 1	26	S.	2
11	19	17	25	0	6	29		5
16	24	17	27	0	10	♏ 7		1
21	29	17	28	♊ ♋	14	13	N.	4
26	♐ 4	17	28	29	18	21		5

M D	W D	Remarkable days, Aſpects, &c.	☉ riſes	☉ ſets	☽'s plac.	☽ riſe & ſets.	☽ ſouth.	Tide
1	5	ALL SAINTS.	6 50	5 10	♈ 18	Morn.	10 36	12
2	6	ALL SOULS.	6 51	5 9	♉ 1	6 16	11 24	1
3	7	7*s ſouth 12 54	6 52	5 8	15	Moon	12 15	2
4	G	21 paſt Trinity.	6 53	5 7	29	riſes	Morn.	3
5	2	POWDER PLOT	6 54	5 6	♊ 13	After.	2 6	3
6	3	☽ with ♂ *Rain*	6 55	5 5	28	7 41	3 5	4
7	4	♄ riſes 11 46	6 56	5 4	♋ 12	8 50	4 2	5
8	5	*about this time*;	6 58	5 2	26	9 55	4 56	6
9	6	□ ☉ ♄ *then plea-*	6 59	5 1	♌ 11	11 1	5 46	7
10	7	*ſant and ſettled*;	7 0	5 0	25	12 10	6 38	8
11	G	22 paſt Trinity.	7 1	4 59	♍ 8	Morn.	7 26	9
12	2	♂ riſes 7 35	7 3	4 57	[illegible]	[illegible]	[illegible]	[illegible]
13	3	Cor ♌ riſes 11,51	7 4	4 56	♎ 6	3 25	9 2	11
14	4	*now clouds with*	7 5	4 55	19	4 28	9 51	11
15	5	Arct. riſes 3 27	7 6	4 54	♏ 3	5 31	10 39	12
16	6	♃ ſ. 6 57 *cold*	7 7	4 53	16	6 32	11 26	1
17	7	B. eye ſo. 12 51	7 8	4 52	29	Moon	12 16	2
18	G	23 paſt Trinity.	7 9	4 51	♐ 11	ſets	After.	3
19	2	7*s ſouth 11,49	7 10	4 50	24	After.	1 55	3
20	3	✶ ♀ ☿ *rain.*	7 11	4 49	♑ 6	7 29	2 13	4
21	4	♂ ſouth 2 16	7 12	4 48	18	8 20	3 24	5
22	5	☌ ♃ ♂ *unſettled*	7 12	4 48	♒ 0	9 23	4 19	6
23	6	*weather.*	7 13	4 47	12	10 12	4 59	7
24	7	Spica ♍ r. 3 46	7 14	4 46	23	11 3	5 37	8
25	G	24 paſt Trinity.	7 15	4 45	♓ 5	12 2	6 19	9
26	2	Day 9h.28 long	7 16	4 44	17	12 57	6 57	9
27	3	♀ ſets 7 45	7 16	4 44	♈ 0	Morn.	7 40	10
28	4	*then moderate.*	7 17	4 43	13	2 55	8 28	11
29	5	7*s ſouth 11, 17	7 18	4 42	26	4 2	9 17	12
30	6	St. ANDREW.	7 18	4 42	♉ 9	5 4	10 6	12

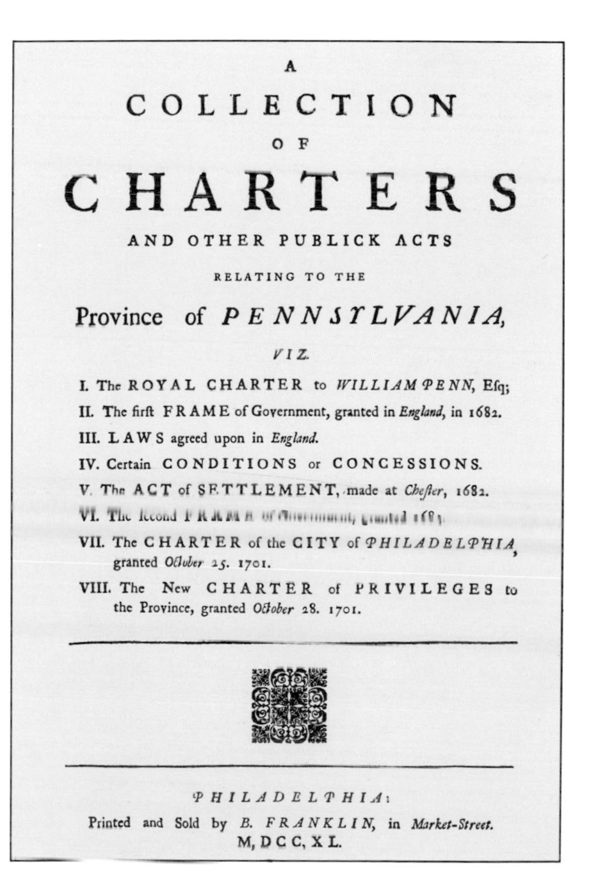
A
COLLECTION
OF
CHARTERS
AND OTHER PUBLICK ACTS
RELATING TO THE
Province of *PENNSYLVANIA*,
VIZ.

I. The ROYAL CHARTER to *WILLIAM PENN*, Eſq;
II. The firſt FRAME of Government, granted in *England*, in 1682.
III. LAWS agreed upon in *England*.
IV. Certain CONDITIONS or CONCESSIONS.
V. The ACT of SETTLEMENT, made at *Cheſter*, 1682.
VI. The ſecond FRAME of Government, granted 1683.
VII. The CHARTER of the CITY of *PHILADELPHIA*, granted *October* 25. 1701.
VIII. The New CHARTER of PRIVILEGES to the Province, granted *October* 28. 1701.

PHILADELPHIA:
Printed and Sold by *B. FRANKLIN*, in *Market-Street.*
M, DCC, XL.

Benjamin Bannecker (left), an African American publisher, was also an amateur astronomer and surveyor (he helped Andrew Ellicott survey the ten-mile square plot for Washington, D.C.). He was much admired by Thomas Jefferson, and for his part, scolded Jefferson for writing the Declaration of Independence and yet still owning slaves.

The New York Weekly Journal *(below, left) was published by John Peter Zenger, an early advocate of freedom of the press. It provided readers with a synopsis of European and domestic news. The* American Magazine *(bottom right) was one of several monthlies published in Boston in the mid-eighteenth century. It was a journal of opinions and essays rather than news.*

Numb. L.

THE

New-York Weekly JOURNAL.

Containing the freshest Advices, Foreign, and Domestick.

MUNDAY October 14*th*, 1734.

Mr. *Zenger*;

I Have been Reading, the arguments of Mr. *Smith*, and *Murray*, with Regard to the Courts, and there is one Thing, I can't comprehend, *viz.* If it is the same Court, I take it, that all the Writs ought to be taken out in *England*, and tested by the Judges there; if they are taken out here, the same Judges ought to test them here. If it is a like Court, it is not the same; and if not the same, it is not that fundamental Court which is established by immemorial Custom. I would be glad some of your Correspondents would clear up this Point; because in my poor Oppinion, if the Exchequer Court here is not the same identical Court as the Exchequer Court in *England*, it is without Lawful Authority.

FOREIGN AFFAIRS.

Dantzick, August 4.

Yesterday the Bishop of Cracow, in the King's Name, received Homage of this City, and the Ceremony was very magnificent. His Majesty, before his Departure, issued the Universalia for holding of the Petty-Dyets in the Provinces. Those in Polish Prussia, will be held in 15 Days. The Russian and Saxon Troops will march suddenly to the Places where the Provincial Assemblies are to be opened; and the rest are to go and post themselves in Great Poland. M. Rewuski, the Crown Carver, is declared Regimentary, and is to command a Body of Troops, consisting of 2000 Russian Dragoons, 11000 Cossacks, and the Regiment Guards formerly in the Service of King Stanislaus.

Brussels, August 6.

Letters from Rome of the 17*th* past advise. That they had Advice there that the Siege of Gaeta was not yet formed, altho' the Spaniards had there 70 Cannon, and Mortars, and were working on Batteries, but that all they raised in the Night was beat down next Morning by the Cannon of the Palace; and that the Heats being already Excessive, the Spaniards were in Fear of loosing a vast Number of Men in the Reduction of that Fortress.

Hamburg, August 10.

According to Letters from the Camp before Dantzick, the Vessels there were taken up by Order of the Generals in Chief, to serve for carrying the heavy Artillery and Baggage by Water to Thorn and Warsaw.

We have certain Advice, that King, Stanislaus was departed from Brandenburg Prussia, and arrived safe in the Crown Army, under the Command of M. Kiowski, near Peterkow the 24*th* past, and immediately afterwards held a Council of War, wherein it was resolved to draw all the dispersed Troops into a Body, and march directly to Volhinia in Podolia.

Amst.

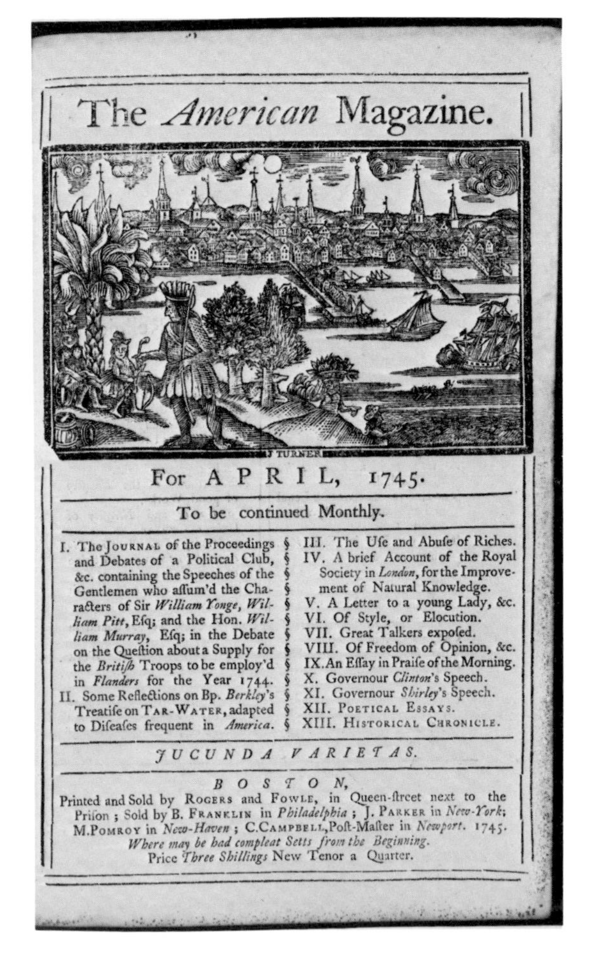

The *American* Magazine.

For APRIL, 1745.

To be continued Monthly.

I. The JOURNAL of the Proceedings and Debates of a Political Club, &c. containing the Speeches of the Gentlemen who assum'd the Characters of Sir *William Yonge*, *William Pitt*, Esq; and the Hon. *William Murray*, Esq; in the Debate on the Question about a Supply for the *British* Troops to be employ'd in *Flanders* for the Year 1744.
II. Some Reflections on Bp. *Berkley*'s Treatise on TAR-WATER, adapted to Diseases frequent in *America*.
III. The Use and Abuse of Riches.
IV. A brief Account of the Royal Society in *London*, for the Improvement of Natural Knowledge.
V. A Letter to a young Lady, &c.
VI. Of Style, or Elocution.
VII. Great Talkers exposed.
VIII. Of Freedom of Opinion, &c.
IX. An Essay in Praise of the Morning.
X. Governour *Clinton*'s Speech.
XI. Governour *Shirley*'s Speech.
XII. POETICAL ESSAYS.
XIII. HISTORICAL CHRONICLE.

JUCUNDA VARIETAS.

BOSTON,

Printed and Sold by ROGERS and FOWLE, in Queen-street next to the Prison; Sold by B. FRANKLIN in *Philadelphia*; J. PARKER in *New-York*; M.POMROY in *New-Haven*; C.CAMPBELL, Post-Master in *Newport*. 1745.

Where may be had compleat Setts from the Beginning.

Price *Three Shillings* New Tenor a Quarter.

THE SENTIMENTS of an
AMERICAN WOMAN.

ON the commencement of actual war, the Women of America manifested a firm resolution to contribute as much as could depend on them, to the deliverance of their country. Animated by the purest patriotism, they are sensible of sorrow at this day, in not offering more than barren wishes for the success of so glorious a Revolution. They aspire to render themselves more really useful; and this sentiment is universal from the north to the south of the Thirteen United States. Our ambition is kindled by the fame of those heroines of antiquity, who have rendered their sex illustrious, and have proved to the universe, that, if the weakness of our Constitution, if opinion and manners did not forbid us to march to glory by the same paths as the Men, we should at least equal, and sometimes surpass them in our love for the public good. I glory in all that which my sex has done great and commendable. I call to mind with enthusiasm and with admiration, all those acts of courage, of constancy and patriotism, which history has transmitted to us: The people favoured by Heaven, preserved from destruction by the virtues, the zeal and the resolution of Deborah, of Judith, of Esther! The fortitude of the mother of the Macchabees, in giving up her sons to die before her eyes: Rome saved from the fury of a victorious enemy by the efforts of Volumnia, and other Roman Ladies: So many famous sieges where the Women have been seen forgetting the weakness of their sex, building new walls, digging trenches with their feeble hands; furnishing arms to their defenders, they themselves darting the missile weapons on the enemy, resigning the ornaments of their apparel, and their fortune, to fill the public treasury, and to hasten the deliverance of their country; burying themselves under its ruins; throwing themselves into the flames rather than submit to the disgrace of humiliation before a proud enemy.

Born for liberty, disdaining to bear the irons of a tyrannic Government, we associate ourselves to the grandeur of those Sovereigns, cherished and revered, who have held with so much splendour the scepter of the greatest States, The Batildas, the Elizabeths, the Maries, the Catharines, who have extended the empire of liberty, and contented to reign by sweetness and justice, have broken the chains of slavery, forged by tyrants in the times of ignorance and barbarity. The Spanish Women, do they not make, at this moment, the most patriotic sacrifices, to encrease the means of victory in the hands of their Sovereign. He is a friend to the French Nation. They are our allies. We call to mind, doubly interested, that it was a French Maid who kindled up amongst her fellow-citizens, the flame of patriotism buried under long misfortunes: It was the Maid of Orleans who drove from the kingdom of France the ancestors of those same British, whose odious yoke we have just shaken off; and whom it is necessary that we drive from this Continent.

But I must limit myself to the recollection of this small number of atchievements. Who knows if persons disposed to censure, and sometimes too severely with regard to us, may not disapprove our appearing acquainted even with the actions of which our sex boasts? We are at least certain, that he cannot be a good citizen who will not applaud our efforts for the relief of the armies which defend our lives, our possessions, our liberty? The situation of our soldiery has been represented to me; the evils inseparable from war, and the firm and generous spirit which has enabled them to support these. But it has been said, that they may apprehend, that, in the course of a long war, the view of their distresses may be lost, and their services be forgotten. Forgotten! never; I can answer in the name of all my sex. Brave Americans, your disinterestedness, your courage, and your constancy will always be dear to America, as long as she shall preserve her virtue.

We know that at a distance from the theatre of war, if we enjoy any tranquility, it is the fruit of your watchings, your labours, your dangers. If I live happy in the midst of my family; if my husband cultivates his field, and reaps his harvest in peace; if, surrounded with my children, I myself nourish the youngest, and press it to my bosom, without being affraid of seeing myself separated from it, by a ferocious enemy; if the house in which we dwell; if our barns, our orchards are safe at the present time from the hands of those incendiaries, it is to you that we owe it. And shall we hesitate to evidence to you our gratitude? Shall we hesitate to wear a cloathing more simple; hair dressed less elegant, while at the price of this small privation, we shall deserve your benedictions. Who, amongst us, will not renounce with the highest pleasure, those vain ornaments, when she shall consider that the valiant defenders of America will be able to draw some advantage from the money which she may have laid out in these; that they will be better defended from the rigours of the seasons, that after their painful toils, they will receive some extraordinary and unexpected relief; that these presents will perhaps be valued by them at a greater price, when they will have it in their power to say: *This is the offering of the Ladies.* The time is arrived to display the same sentiments which animated us at the beginning of the Revolution, when we renounced the use of teas, however agreeable to our taste, rather than receive them from our persecutors; when we made it appear to them that we placed former necessaries in the rank of superfluities, when our liberty was interested; when our republican and laborious hands spun the flax, prepared the linen intended for the use of our soldiers; when exiles and fugitives we supported with courage all the evils which are the concomitants of war. Let us not lose a moment; let us be engaged to offer the homage of our gratitude at the altar of military valour, and you, our brave deliverers, while mercenary slaves combat to cause you to share with them, the irons with which they are loaded, receive with a free hand our offering, the purest which can be presented to your virtue,

BY AN AMERICAN WOMAN.

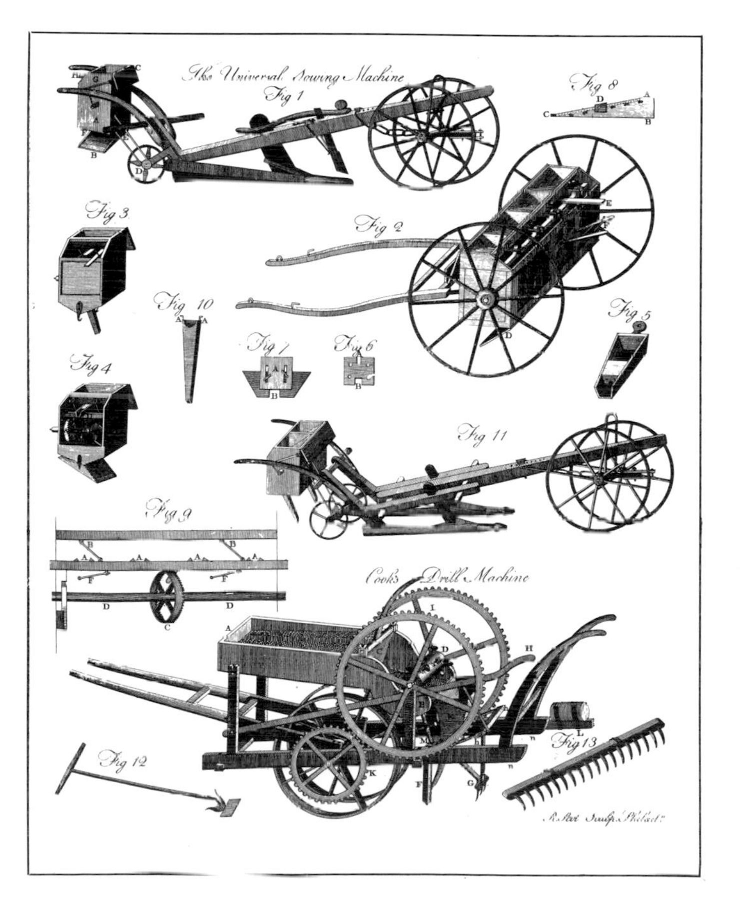

This woodcut (above, right) in The New England Almanack *illustrated an account of the adventures of Hannah Snell. Deserted by her husband, readers were told, she disguised herself as a man, joined the English Navy to find him, and braved hurricanes and war in the process.*

A broadside, like The Sentiments of an American Woman *(above), was a large single sheet of paper on which an appeal or a statement of belief was printed. This one supports the Patriot cause during the American Revolution. The detailed diagrams at right appeared in Dobson's* Encyclopedia, *published in Philadelphia in 1799.*

BANKING AND CURRENCY

An ongoing problem in the colonies was a lack of currency. English law forbade the export of money, and the colonies were not allowed to mint it. They managed as best they could. Tobacco, corn, cattle, and wheat all served, at different times and in different places, as "legal tender." Spanish and Portuguese coins were used, but were called by the names of denominations of English currency—pounds, shillings, and pence. And despite the law, some colonies did coin their own money and print their own bills. Massachusetts was the first colony to issue paper money, in 1690.

To finance the Revolution, the Continental Congress authorized the printing of Continental currency — bills of credit—with a face value of $241.5 million; state bills of credit contributed another $210 million. Interest-bearing bonds known as loan office certificates amounted to $20 million, and requisitions from the states, based on their populations, yielded $5 million in paper money and around $4 million in goods. These sums, together with $2.6 million in contributions (along with a loan of $6.4 million) from France, made up the war chest for the American Revolution.

Robert Morris (above) was appointed superintendent of finance by Congress in February 1781 at a point in the Revolutionary War when the Continental currency was worth less than the paper it was printed on. Morris secured a loan of $200,000 in gold from France (delivered by the French Navy), and on that basis he founded the Bank of North America in November 1781. When independence had been won, Morris, whose contribution to the Revolution had been inestimable, declined an invitation to serve as first secretary of the Treasury.

Several colonies were obliged to mint their own money. Examples of colonial currency (opposite page) include the Pine Tree Shilling, issued by Massachusetts (top, right), and the $65 bill, backed by Spanish "pieces of eight." The soundest colonial currency was Pennsylvania's, organized by Benjamin Franklin.

The first bank in the United States (opposite page, bottom) was built in Philadelphia. This engraving was published by William Birch and Sons in 1799.

THE UNITED STATES

No. 5135 Sixty-five Dollars.

THE Bearer is entitled to receive Sixty-five Spanish milled Dollars, or an equal Sum in Gold or Silver, according to a Resolution of CONGRESS of the 14th January, 1779.

FIAT JUSTITIA

LXV DOLLARS.

THE UNITED STATES

No. 307061 Forty Dollars.

This BILL entitles the Bearer to receive Forty Spanish milled Dollars, or the Value thereof in Gold or Silver, according to a Resolution passed by Congress at Philadelphia, Sept. 26th, 1778.

CONFEDERATION

XL DOLLARS.

TRADES IN THE DECORATIVE ARTS

Craftspeople created many useful products, but some, especially cabinetmakers and joiners, also created works of art. Few colonists brought furniture with them when they crossed the Atlantic. For most, the shipping costs were far too expensive and in any case there was plenty of good wood in the New World, just waiting to be made into furniture. Thus cabinetmaking got a colonial head start.

Pewter, an alloy of tin, lead, and either copper, antimony, or bismuth, was known as "poor man's silver." It was a popular item in the colonies, because a tankard, say, could be easily melted down and refashioned into something else, like a platter. Silversmiths (who also worked with pewter) were kept busy because silver was both beautiful and a good way for people to secure their wealth in a nation without banks.

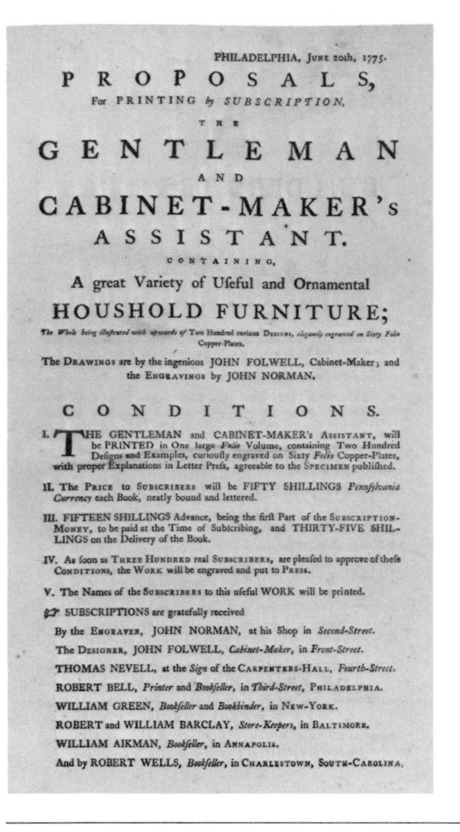

PHILADELPHIA, June 20th, 1775.

PROPOSALS,

For PRINTING *by SUBSCRIPTION*,

THE

GENTLEMAN

AND

CABINET-MAKER's

ASSISTANT.

CONTAINING,

A great Variety of Uſeful and Ornamental

HOUSHOLD FURNITURE;

The Whole being illuſtrated with upwards of Two Hundred curious Designs, *elegantly engraved on Sixty Folio* Copper-Plates.

The Drawings are by the ingenious JOHN FOLWELL, Cabinet-Maker; and the Engravings by JOHN NORMAN.

CONDITIONS.

I. THE GENTLEMAN and CABINET-MAKER's Assistant, will be PRINTED in One large *Folio* Volume, containing Two Hundred Deſigns and Examples, curiouſly engraved on Sixty *Folio* Copper-Plates, with proper Explanations in Letter Preſs, agreeable to the Specimen publiſhed.

II. The Price to Subscribers will be FIFTY SHILLINGS *Pennſylvania Currency* each Book, neatly bound and lettered.

III. FIFTEEN SHILLINGS Advance, being the firſt Part of the Subscription-Money, to be paid at the Time of Subſcribing, and THIRTY-FIVE SHILLINGS on the Delivery of the Book.

IV. As ſoon as Three Hundred real Subscribers, are pleaſed to approve of theſe Conditions, the Work will be engraved and put to Press.

V. The Names of the Subscribers to this uſeful WORK will be printed.

☞ SUBSCRIPTIONS are gratefully received

By the Engraver, JOHN NORMAN, at his Shop in *Second-Street*.

The Designer, JOHN FOLWELL, *Cabinet-Maker*, in *Front-Street*.

THOMAS NEVELL, at the *Sign* of the Carpenters-Hall, *Fourth-Street*.

ROBERT BELL, *Printer* and *Bookſeller*, in *Third-Street*, Philadelphia.

WILLIAM GREEN, *Bookſeller* and *Bookbinder*, in New-York.

ROBERT and WILLIAM BARCLAY, *Store-Keepers*, in Baltimore.

WILLIAM AIKMAN, *Bookſeller*, in Annapolis.

And by ROBERT WELLS, *Bookſeller*, in Charlestown, South-Carolina.

Above: An advertisement seeking to finance the publication of a book of fine furniture designs, modeled on Thomas Chippendale's influential The Gentleman and Cabinet-maker's Director. *Below: A pewter tankard with a tight-fitting lid, and (left) a pewter works, where such a vessel would have been made. The large wheel at the rear of the shop drives the bellows that make the furnace burn hot.*

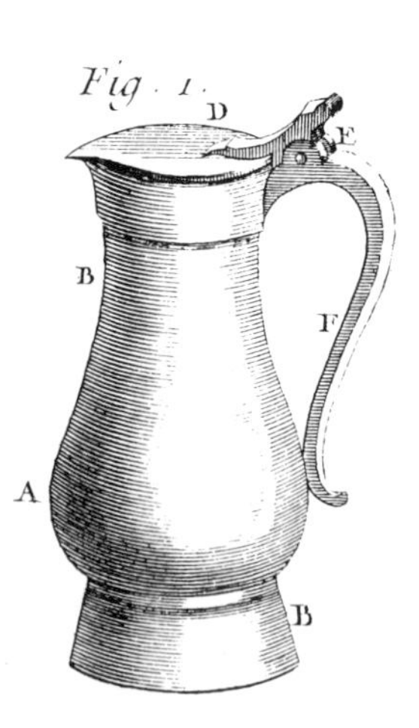

Above, left: A chair in the popular Chippendale style, probably made in Philadelphia, where, before the Revolution, there were at least twenty-nine copies of Chippendale's influential book of furniture designs. Above, right: A furniture maker's shop, where the skills of the cabinetmaker, joiner, and upholsterer were all essential. Below: A silversmith's shop. Whereas pewter was commonly shaped in molds, silver was primarily worked with a hammer.

FIRE FIGHTING IN COLONIAL CITIES

Fire was a constant hazard in all colonial cities, and when it broke out the results were often catastrophic. City fires quickly got out of control for three reasons. First, most buildings were made of wood, and were highly flammable. Second, buildings usually stood close together, so when a fire did break out, it tended to spread rapidly. Third, water was scarce in most colonial cities, even for drinking and washing, and many fires raged because there was simply no water for putting them out.

The most common method of fire fighting was the bucket brigade: a chain of people passing buckets of water from a pump or pond to the site of the fire. Sometimes a water cart equipped with its own hand-driven pumps (the forerunner of the modern fire engine) would be brought to the fire.

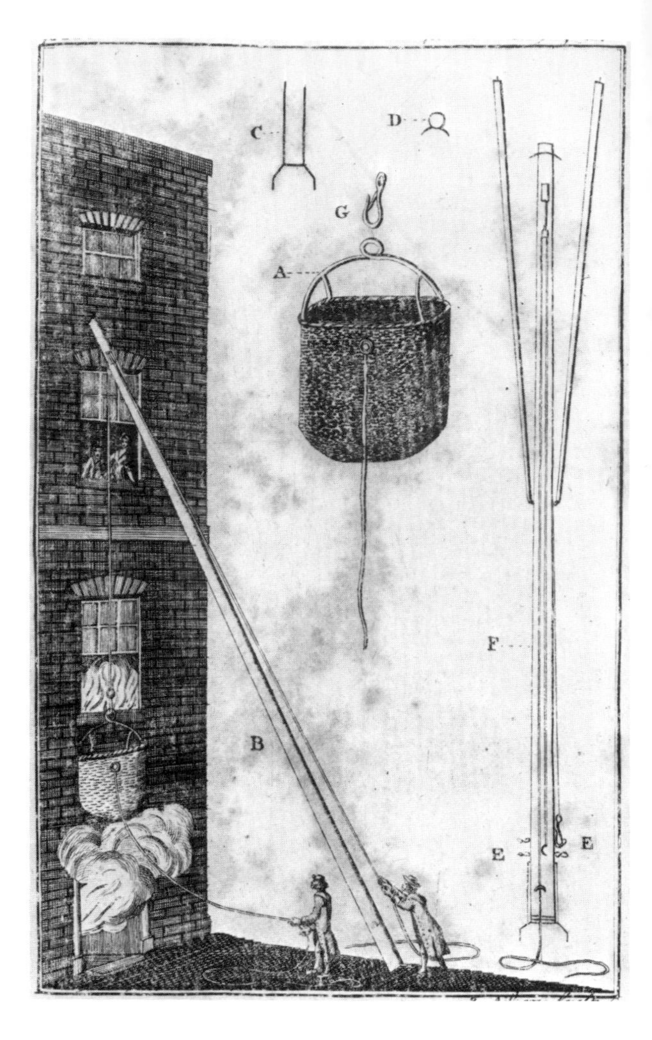

Colonial fire-fighting equipment: The basket-and-ladder system was used to lower a person to safety from an upper story. For the greatest possible safety from fire, some households owned their own "hand engine," a mini-pumper that was kept primed with water, and, advertisements said, could "throwe Water with ease 40 feet perpendicular." The pump, which sold for twenty-five shillings, was also recommended as "very proper for Coasters to carry to sea to wet the Sails in small Winds to preserve them from Mildews."

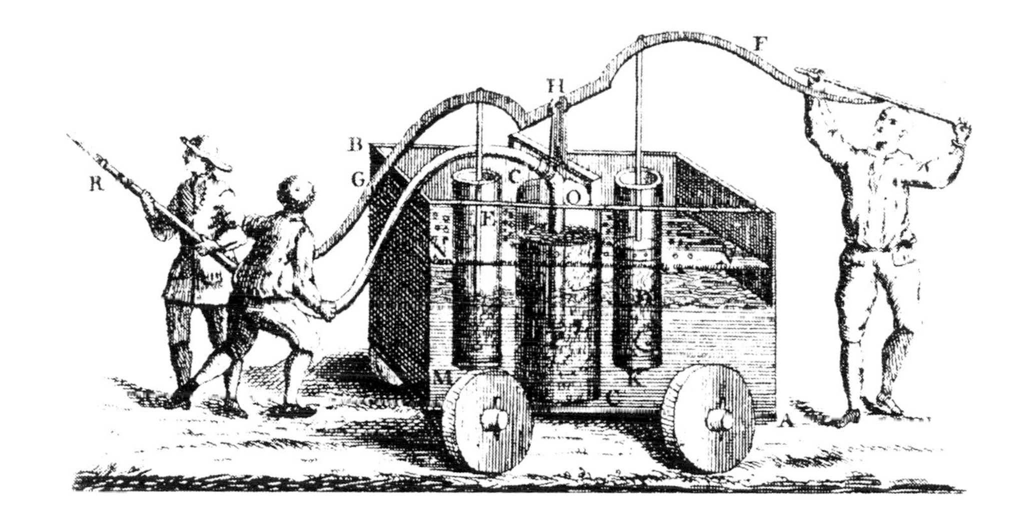

Above: The forerunner of the fire engine. Below: The kind of fire it had to deal with. The illustration shows perhaps the worst fire in colonial history, which began in New York on September 21, 1776, and destroyed a quarter of the city. Some say the fire was set by the British, and some say that Patriots were responsible. Others say the fire was purely accidental.

CRIME AND PUNISHMENT IN THE COLONIES

For the first ten years of its existence, the Massachusetts Bay Colony had no criminal code. Crimes were defined, and punishments decreed, by the Court of Assistants, whose members were known as magistrates. In 1635 the colonists demanded that a code of written laws be compiled, but it was 1641 before the code (known as the Body of Liberties) was established. Like other Puritan law codes, it relied heavily upon the Bible, and very little on the body of English common law. It also admitted the curious and medieval trial by ordeal. One of the strangest of these was the ordeal by touch, which rested on the belief that if a murderer touched his victim's body it would begin to bleed. As late as 1769 two suspects in the murder of a young mother were invited to prove their innocence by performing this ordeal, and the body was publicly exhumed for that purpose, five weeks after its burial. The suspects refused the test, and were brought to trial. John Adams (subsequently president of the United States) served as their defense attorney, and they were acquitted.

At A COVNCIL
Held at Boston the 9th. of April, 1677

THe COVNCIL being informed, that among other Evils that are prevailing among us, in this day of our Calamity, there is practised by some that vanity of Horse racing, for mony, or monyes worth, thereby occasioning much misspence of pretious time, and the drawing of many persons from the duty of their particular Callings, with the hazard of their Limbs and Lives.

It is hereby Ordered that henceforth it shall not be Lawful for any persons to do or practise in that kind, within *four miles* of any Town, or in any *High-way* or *Common Rode*, on penalty of forfieting *twenty Shillings* apiece, nor shall any Game or run in that kind for any mony, or monyes worth upon penalty of forfieting Treble the value thereof, one half to the *party informing*, and the other half to the *Treasury*, nor shall any accompany or abbett any in that practice on the like penalty, and this to continue til the General Courtt take further Order.

And all *Constables* respectively are hereby injoyned to present the Names of all such as shall be found transgressing, contrary to this Order to the *Magistrate*.

Dated the *ninth of April*, 1677.

By the Council
Edward Rawson Sec.

By twentieth-century standards, many ordinances of colonial law were petty and interfering. For example, it was an offense to declare a minister's sermon uninspiring, or to walk in the garden on Sunday. And by today's standards, penalties were cruel. For more serious crimes, ears were cut off, noses were slit, and holes were bored in tongues. Adultery was a capital offense, and carried with it the death penalty. The Puritans believed that horse racing and gambling on horse races were evils which caused people to waste their time, diverted them from their proper duties, and posed dangers to life and limb. The proclamation above, declared by the Boston Council in April 1677, banned all racing and gambling within four miles of any town, road, or highway. For other crimes, people were exposed to public ridicule (opposite page, top), hanged in public (opposite, middle), or jailed. Opposite page, bottom: A jail in Philadelphia.

THE WESTERN FRONTIER

By 1800, settlers had pushed as far west as the Mississippi River. From a few towns and villages along the Atlantic coast, the new nation had grown mightily, and established itself as a free nation in a new land. Before long, Thomas Jefferson's Louisiana Purchase would add more lands to the territories of the United States, and still wider frontiers would be open to settlement and exploration.

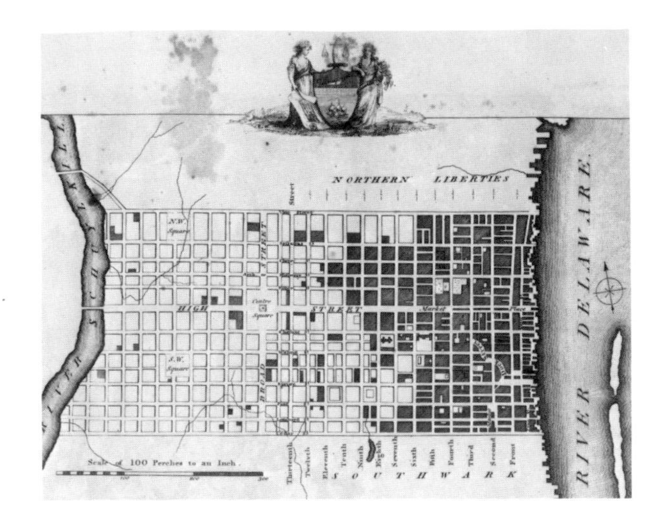

As cities coninued to grow in size and population, more and more citizens considered moving west. The prospect of owning land was especially attractive. This plan of Philadelphia (above) indicates the limited size of private land plots.

Several territories were made into states in the 1790s, including Vermont, Kentucky, and Tennessee. As the country expanded westward, the desire to claim unsettled land grew. This map (opposite page) shows the United States in 1800.

This engraving by William Birch (below) shows a street in Philadelphia in 1799.

TERRITORY
Quebec
Montreal
Canada
NEW YORK
Albany
Windsor
N.HAM.
Boston
CONN.
Hartford
Newport
New Haven
New York
PENNSYLVANIA
Lancaster
Trenton
Philadelphia
JERSEY
Annapolis
D.C.
MD.
Washington
VIRGINIA
Richmond
Norfolk
Chillicothe
Cincinnati
Frankfort
Louisville
KENTUCKY
Vincennes
Kaskaskia
INDIANA TERRITORY
(1800)
NORTHWEST
Detroit
Knoxville
Nashville
TENNESSEE
NORTH CAROLINA
Raleigh
SOUTH CAROLINA
Columbia
Disputed by United States and Georgia
GEORGIA
Louisville
Savannah
MISSISSIPPI TERRITORY
WEST FLORIDA
EAST FLORIDA
St. Augustine
Mobile
New Orleans
Spanish
GULF OF MEXICO
ATLANTIC OCEAN
BAHAMA ISLANDS
Longitude West from Greenwich

Resource Guide

Key to picture positions: (T) top, (C) center, (B) bottom; and in combinations: (TL) top left, (TC) top center, (TR) top right, (BL) bottom left, (BC) bottom center, (BR) bottom right, (CR) center right, (CL) center left.

Key to picture locations within the Library of Congress collections (and where available, photo-negative numbers): P - Prints and Photographs; HABS - Historical American Buildings Survey (div. of Prints and Photographs); R - Rare Book Division; G - General Collections; MSS - Manuscript Division; G&M - Geography and Map Division.

PICTURES IN THIS VOLUME

2-3 farmyard, P, USZ62-31133 **4-5** woodcut, P, USZ62-32576 **6-7** printing shop, P, USZ62-87781

Timeline: **8** T, Columbus, G; CL, Pope Alexander, P, USZ62-49700; CR, totem, G; BL, Las Casas, G; BR, Smith, P, USZ62-31735 **9** T, Shakespeare, G; CL, seal, G; CR, fort, P, USZ62-5139; B, Pocahontas, P, USZ62-39316 **10** T, fire, G; C, Locke, G; B, shilling, G **11** T, Louis XIV, G; C, Philip, P, USZ62-96234; B, post-boy, G **12** TL, Marlborough, G; TR, seal, P, USZ62-676; C, cottage, P, USZ62-33762 **13** T, Swift, G; C, trial, G **14** TL, Frederick, G; TR, Rousseau, G; C, cartoon, P, USZ62-9701; B, sugar mill, R **15** TL, Lavoisier, G; TR, Bastille, G; C, Washington, P, USZ62-45479

Part I: **16-17** farm, P, USZ62-31149 **18-19** TL, village, P, USZ62-367; C, map, G **20-21** TL, deer, P; TR, gold, P; BR, boat, P **22-23** TL, fort, P; BL, cooking, P; TR, broadside, MSS; BR, colonists, G **24-25** TL, cradle, P; C, plantation, P, USZ62-17899 **26-27** TL, Puritans, P, USZ62-34139; TR, house, P, USZ62-34142; BR, chair, P **28-29** TL, Miles Standish, P, USZ62-3946; BL, farm, P, USZ62-32577; TR, family, P, USZ62-54384; BR, women, S **30-31** TL, onion farm, G; C, settlement farm, P, USZ62-31185 **32-33** TL, farmyard, P, USZ62-31153; TR, title page, R **34-35** C, tobacco, G; TR, slaves, P, USZ62-53345 **36-37** TL, manufacture, P, USZ62-29058; TR, wharf, P, USZ62-20127A; BR, transport, P, USZ62-12865 **38-39** TL, letter, MSS; BL, cave dwelling, R; TR, trading, G; BR, Quaker, R **40-41** TL, hay, R; BL, threshing, R; TR, butter, R; BR, cheese, R **42-43** TL, oxen, P, USZ62-31150; BL, Green Hill, P, USZ62-31787; TR, granary, P, USZ62-31152 **44-45** TL, flax, P, USZ62-14838; BL, spinning wheel, P, USZ62-56781; TR, manufacture, P, USZ62-51022 **46-47** TL, letter, MSS; BL, silkworms, P, USZ62-49632; TR, house, G; BR, silk plate, R **48-49** TL, saltworks, P, USZ62-31144; TR, gristmill, R; BR, sawmill, P, USZ62-45548 **50-51** TL, fishing stages, G; BL, New Jersey, P, USZ62-50795; TR, fishing net, R; BR, whale, G **52-53** TL, Washington, G; TR, map, P, USZ62-5937; BR, wedding, R

Part II: **54-55** Alms house, P, USZ62-56358 **56-57** TL, St. Augustine, P, USZ62-053276; TR, map, G **58-59** C, Baltimore, P, USZ62-31953; TR, Williamsburg, P, USZ62-2104 **60-61** TL, Bethlehem, P; BL, glass, P, USZ62-52174; BC, potters, R; TC, post-boy, G; TR, peddler, G; BR, tinsmith, R **62-63** TL, plan, P, USZ62-45597; BL, map, P, USZ62-45598; TR, water front, R; BR, buildings, G **64-65** TC, cooking, R; TR, shopping, R; BR, marketplace, P, USZ62-3239 **66-67** TL, children, G; BL, dancing, P, USZ62-33939; TR, horseracing, G; C, boules, R; BR, billards, P, USZ62-20404 **68-69** TL, horse, R; BL, coach, P, USZ62-5675; TR, blacksmith, R; BR, coachmakers, R **70-71** C, Boston, P, USZ62-1504; TR, Mechanicks, P, USZ62-59808 **72-73** TL, house builders, R; TR, house, G **74-75** TL, shoemaker, R; BL, tailor, R; TR, Faneuil Hall, P, USZ62-2178; BR, tavern, G **76-77** BL, fashions, G; TR, hairdo, G; BR, ship, P, USZ62-3236 **78-79** TL, sloop, G; BL, lighthouse, P, USZ62-31786; TR, shipbuilding, P, USZ62-56362; BR, ropeworks, R **80-81** TL, Franklin, G; BL, printing press, P, USZ62-87784; TR, card, G; BC, almanac, P, USZ62-44844; BR, charters, MSS **82-83** TL, Banneker, G; BL, *NY Weekly Journal*, S; BC, *American Magazine*, S; TC, American Woman, MSS; TR, Hannah Snell, P, USZ62-49995; BR, Dobson Ency., G **84-85** TL, Morris, G; TR, coins, G; C, dollar, R; BR, bank, P, USZ62-56384 **86-87** TL, advertisement, R; BL, pewter maker, R; BC, jug, R; TC, chair, P, USZ62-92877; TR, cabinetmaker, R; BR, silversmith, R **88-89** TL, bucket, P, USZ62-31145; TR, fire engine, G; BR, fire, P,USZ62-42 **90-91** TL, broadside, MSS; TR, stocks, G; CR, hanging, G; BR, jail, P, USZ62-56357 **92-93** TL, plan, P, USZ62-56335; BL, Philadelphia, P, USZ62-56351; TR, map, G

SUGGESTED READING

BRIDENBAUGH, CARL. *The Colonial Craftsman.* New York: Dover, 1990.

DOW, GEORGE F. *Daily Life in the Massachusetts Bay Colony.* New York: Dover, 1988.

HAWKE, DAVID F. *Everyday Life in Early America.* New York: Harper and Row, 1988.

MORRISON, SAMUEL E. *The Oxford History of the American People.* New York: Oxford University Press, 1965.

SMITH, BARBARA C. *After the Revolution: The Smithsonian History of Everyday Life in the Eighteenth Century.* New York: Pantheon, 1985.

Index

Page numbers in *italics* indicate illustrations.